INDIAN COOKBOOK 2022

TRADITIONAL AND TASTY INDIAN RECIPES

MELANIA JORDAN

Table of Contents

Garlic Raita 19
    Ingredients 19
    Method 19
Mixed Vegetable Raita 20
    Ingredients 20
    Method 20
Boondi Raita 21
    Ingredients 21
    Method 21
Cauliflower Raita 22
    Ingredients 22
    Method 23
Cabbage Raita 24
    Ingredients 24
    Method 24
Beetroot Raita 25
    Ingredients 25
    Method 25
Sprouted Pulses Raita 26
    Ingredients 26
    Method 26
Pasta Pudina Raita 27
    Ingredients 27

- Method 27
- Mint Raita 28
  - Ingredients 28
  - Method 28
- Aubergine Raita 29
  - Ingredients 29
  - Method 29
- Saffron Raita 30
  - Ingredients 30
  - Method 30
- Yam Raita 31
  - Ingredients 31
  - Method 32
- Okra Raita 33
  - Ingredients 33
  - Method 33
- Crunchy Spinach Patty 34
  - Ingredients 34
  - Method 34
- Rava Dosa 36
  - Ingredients 36
  - Method 36
- Doodhi Cutlet 37
  - Ingredients 37
  - For the white sauce: 37
  - Method 37
- Patra 39

- Ingredients 39
  - For the batter: 39
  - Method 40
- Nargisi Chicken Kebab 41
  - Ingredients 41
  - Method 42
- Sev Puris with Savoury Topping 43
  - Ingredients 43
  - Method 44
- Special Roll 45
  - Ingredients 45
  - Method 46
- Fried Colocasia 47
  - Ingredients 47
  - Method 48
- Mixed Dhal Dosa 49
  - Ingredients 49
  - Method 49
- Makkai Cakes 50
  - Ingredients 50
  - Method 51
- Hara Bhara Kebab 52
  - Ingredients 52
  - Method 52
- Fish Pakoda 54
  - Ingredients 54
  - Method 55

- Shammi Kebab 56
  - Ingredients 56
  - Method 57
- Basic Dhokla 58
  - Ingredients 58
  - Method 59
- Adai 60
  - Ingredients 60
  - Method 61
- Double Decker Dhokla 62
  - Ingredients 62
  - Method 63
- Ulundu Vada 64
  - Ingredients 64
  - Method 64
- Bhakar Wadi 65
  - Ingredients 65
  - Method 65
- Mangalorean Chaat 67
  - Ingredients 67
  - Method 68
- Pani Puri 69
  - Ingredients 69
  - For the stuffing: 69
  - For the pani: 69
  - Method 70
- Stuffed Spinach Egg 71

    Ingredients 71

    Method 72

Sada Dosa 73

    Ingredients 73

    Method 73

Potato Samosa 75

    Ingredients 75

    Method 76

Hot Kachori 77

    Ingredients 77

    Method 77

Khandvi 79

    Ingredients 79

    Method 80

Makkai Squares 81

    Ingredients 81

    Method 82

Dhal Pakwan 83

    Ingredients 83

    For the pakwan: 83

    Method 84

Spicy Sev 85

    Ingredients 85

    Method 85

Stuffed Veggie Crescents 86

    Ingredients 86

    For the filling: 86

- Method 87
- Kachori Usal 88
  - Ingredients 88
  - For the filling: 88
  - For the sauce: 89
  - Method 89
- Dhal Dhokli 91
  - Ingredients 91
  - For the dhal: 91
  - Method 92
- Misal 93
  - Ingredients 93
  - For the spice mixture: 94
  - Method 95
- Pandori 96
  - Ingredients 96
  - Method 96
- Vegetable Adai 97
  - Ingredients 97
  - Method 98
- Spicy Corn on the Cob 99
  - Ingredients 99
  - Method 99
- Mixed Vegetable Chop 100
  - Ingredients 100
  - Method 101
- Idli Upma 102

Ingredients	102
Method	103
Dhal Bhajiya	104
Ingredients	104
Method	104
Masala Papad	105
Ingredients	105
Method	105
Vegetable Sandwich	106
Ingredients	106
Method	106
Sprouted Mung Bean Rolls	107
Ingredients	107
Method	108
Chutney Sandwich	109
Ingredients	109
Method	109
Chatpata Gobhi	110
Ingredients	110
Method	110
Sabudana Vada	111
Ingredients	111
Method	111
Bread Upma	112
Ingredients	112
Method	113
Spicy Khaja	114

- Ingredients ... 114
  - Method ... 115
- Crispy Potato ... 116
  - Ingredients ... 116
  - Method ... 117
- Dhal Vada ... 118
  - Ingredients ... 118
  - Method ... 119
- Batter Fried Shrimp ... 120
  - Ingredients ... 120
  - Method ... 121
- Mackerel in Tomato Gravy ... 122
  - Ingredients ... 122
  - Method ... 123
- Konju Ullaruathu ... 124
  - Ingredients ... 124
  - Method ... 125
- Chemeen Manga Curry ... 126
  - Ingredients ... 126
  - Method ... 127
- Simple Machchi Fry ... 128
  - Ingredients ... 128
  - Method ... 128
- Machher Kalia ... 129
  - Ingredients ... 129
  - Method ... 130
- Fish Fried in Egg ... 131

- Ingredients 131
- Method 131
- Lau Chingri 132
  - Ingredients 132
  - Method 133
- Tomato Fish 134
  - Ingredients 134
  - Method 135
- Chingri Machher Kalia 136
  - Ingredients 136
  - Method 136
- Fish Tikka Kebab 137
  - Ingredients 137
  - Method 137
- Vegetable Patties 138
  - Ingredients 138
  - Method 138
- Sprouted Beans Bhel 140
  - Ingredients 140
  - For the garnish: 140
  - Method 141
- Aloo Kachori 142
  - Ingredients 142
  - Method 142
- Diet Dosa 143
  - Ingredients 143
  - Method 143

Nutri Roll 145
    Ingredients 145
    Method 146
Sabudana Palak Doodhi Uttapam 147
    Ingredients 147
    Method 148
Poha 149
    Ingredients 149
    Method 150
Vegetable Cutlet 151
    Ingredients 151
    Method 152
Soy Bean Uppit 153
    Ingredients 153
    Method 154
Upma 155
    Ingredients 155
    Method 156
Vermicelli Upma 157
    Ingredients 157
    Method 158
Bonda 159
    Ingredients 159
    Method 160
Instant Dhokla 161
    Ingredients 161
    Method 162

Dhal Maharani 163
    Ingredients 163
        Method 164
Milagu Kuzhambu 165
    Ingredients 165
        Method 166
Dhal Hariyali 167
    Ingredients 167
        Method 168
Dhalcha 169
    Ingredients 169
        Method 170
Tarkari Dhalcha 171
    Ingredients 171
        Method 172
Dhokar Dhalna 173
    Ingredients 173
        Method 173
Varan 175
    Ingredients 175
        Method 175
Sweet Dhal 176
    Ingredients 176
        Method 177
Sweet & Sour Dhal 178
    Ingredients 178
        Method 179

- Mung-ni-Dhal 180
  - Ingredients 180
  - Method 181
- Dhal with Onion & Coconut 182
  - Ingredients 182
  - Method 183
- Dahi Kadhi 184
  - Ingredients 184
  - Method 185
- Spinach Dhal 186
  - Ingredients 186
  - Method 187
- Tawker Dhal 188
  - Ingredients 188
  - Method 189
- Basic Dhal 190
  - Ingredients 190
  - Method 191
- Maa-ki-Dhal 192
  - Ingredients 192
  - Method 193
- Dhansak 194
  - Ingredients 194
  - For the dhal mixture: 194
  - Method 195
- Masoor Dhal 196
  - Ingredients 196

Method	196
Panchemel Dhal	197
Ingredients	197
Method	198
Cholar Dhal	199
Ingredients	199
Method	200
Dilpasand Dhal	201
Ingredients	201
Method	202
Dhal Masoor	203
Ingredients	203
Method	204
Dhal with Aubergine	205
Ingredients	205
Method	206
Yellow Dhal Tadka	207
Ingredients	207
Method	207
Rasam	208
Ingredients	208
For the spice mixture:	208
Method	209
Simple Mung Dhal	210
Ingredients	210
Method	210
Whole Green Mung	211

- Ingredients 211
- Method 212
- Dahi Kadhi with Pakoras 213
  - Ingredients 213
  - For the kadhi: 213
  - Method 214
- Sweet Unripe Mango Dhal 215
  - Ingredients 215
  - Method 216
- Malai Dhal 217
  - Ingredients 217
  - Method 218

Introduction

Indian food varies enormously. Whatever type of food you might be interested in – meat, fish or vegetarian – you will find a recipe to suit your palate and mood. While curry is inevitably associated with India, this term is simply used for meats or vegetables cooked in a spicy sauce, usually eaten with rice or Indian breads. As this collection of a thousand Indian recipes will show you, Indian food is not limited to the familiar restaurant favorites.

Food is taken very seriously in India and cooking is considered an art. Each Indian state has its own traditions, culture, lifestyle and food. Even individual households may have their own secret recipes for the powders and pastes that form the backbone of the dish. However, what all Indian dishes have in common is the delicate alchemy of spices that gives them their characteristic flavor.

The recipes in the book are authentic, such as you might encounter in an Indian home – yet they are simple, so if this is the first time that you are going to cook Indian food, relax. All you need to do is turn the pages, pick what tickles your fancy, and create a delicious meal, the Indian way!

Garlic Raita

Serves 4

Ingredients

2 green chillies

5 garlic cloves

450g/1lb yoghurt, whisked

Salt to taste

Method

- Dry roast the chillies till they turn light brown. Grind them with the garlic.
- Mix with the remaining ingredients. Serve chilled.

Mixed Vegetable Raita

Serves 4

Ingredients

1 large potato, finely diced and boiled

25g/scant 1oz French beans, finely diced and boiled

25g/scant 1oz carrots, finely diced and boiled

50g/1¾oz boiled peas

450g/1lb yoghurt

½ tsp ground black pepper

1 tbsp coriander leaves, finely chopped

Salt to taste

Method

- Mix all the ingredients well in a bowl. Serve chilled.

Boondi Raita

Serves 4

Ingredients

115g/4oz salted boondi*

450g/1lb yoghurt

½ tsp sugar

½ tsp chaat masala*

Method

- Mix all the ingredients well in a bowl. Serve chilled.

Cauliflower Raita

Serves 4

Ingredients

250g/9oz cauliflower, chopped into tiny florets, or grated

Salt to taste

½ tsp ground black pepper

½ tsp chilli powder

½ tsp ground mustard

450g/1lb yoghurt

1 tsp ghee

½ tsp mustard seeds

Chaat masala* to taste

Method
- Mix the cauliflower with salt and steam mixture.
- Whisk the pepper, chilli powder, mustard, salt and yoghurt in a bowl.
- Add the cauliflower mixture to the yoghurt mixture and set aside.
- Heat the ghee in a small saucepan. When it begins to smoke, add the mustard seeds. Let them splutter for 15 seconds.
- Add this with the chaat masala to the yoghurt mixture. Serve chilled.

Cabbage Raita

Serves 4

Ingredients

100g/3½oz cabbage, grated

Salt to taste

1 tbsp coriander leaves, finely chopped

2 tsp grated coconut

450g/1lb yoghurt

1 tsp oil

½ tsp mustard seeds

3-4 curry leaves

Method

- Steam the cabbage with salt. Let it cool down.
- Add the coriander leaves, coconut and yoghurt. Mix well. Set aside.
- Heat the oil in a small saucepan. Add the mustard seeds and curry leaves. Let them splutter for 15 seconds.
- Pour this in the yoghurt mixture. Serve chilled.

Beetroot Raita

Serves 4

Ingredients

1 large beetroot, boiled and grated

450g/1lb yoghurt

½ tsp sugar

Salt to taste

1 tsp ghee

½ tsp cumin seeds

1 green chilli, slit lengthways

1 tbsp coriander leaves, finely chopped

Method

- Mix the beetroot, yoghurt, sugar and salt in a bowl.
- Heat the ghee in a saucepan. Add the cumin seeds and green chilli. Let them splutter for 15 seconds. Add this to the beetroot-yoghurt mixture.
- Transfer to a serving bowl and garnish with the coriander leaves.
- Serve chilled.

Sprouted Pulses Raita

Serves 4

Ingredients

75g/2½oz bean sprouts

75g/2½oz sprouted kaala chana*

75g/2½oz sprouted chickpeas

1 cucumber, finely chopped

10g/¼oz coriander leaves, finely chopped

2 tsp chaat masala*

½ tsp sugar

450g/1lb yoghurt

Method

- Steam the bean sprouts for 5 minutes. Set aside.
- Boil the kaala chana and chickpeas along with some water on a medium heat in a saucepan for 30 minutes. Set aside.
- Mix the bean sprouts with all the remaining ingredients. Mix well. Drain and add the kaala chana and chickpeas.
- Serve chilled.

Pasta Pudina Raita

Serves 4

Ingredients

200g/7oz pasta, boiled

1 large cucumber, finely chopped

450g/1lb yoghurt, whisked

2 tsp ready-made mustard

50g/1¾oz mint leaves, finely chopped

Salt to taste

Method

- Mix all the ingredients together. Serve chilled.

Mint Raita

Serves 4

Ingredients

50g/1¾oz mint leaves

25g/scant 1oz coriander leaves

1 green chilli

2 garlic cloves

450g/1lb yoghurt

1 tsp chaat masala*

1 tsp caster sugar

Salt to taste

Method

- Grind together the mint leaves, coriander leaves, green chilli and garlic.
- Mix with the other ingredients in a bowl.
- Serve chilled.

Aubergine Raita

Serves 4

Ingredients

1 large aubergine

450g/1lb yoghurt

1 large onion, finely grated

2 green chillies, finely chopped

10g/¼oz coriander leaves, finely chopped

Salt to taste

Method

- Pierce the aubergine all over with a fork. Roast in the oven at 180ºC (350ºF, Gas Mark 4) turning it occasionally, till the skin is charred.
- Soak the aubergine in a bowl of water to cool it down. Drain the water and peel off the aubergine skin.
- Mash the aubergine till smooth. Mix with all the other ingredients.
- Serve chilled.

Saffron Raita

Serves 4

Ingredients

350g/12oz yoghurt

1 tsp saffron, soaked in 2 tbsp milk for 30 minutes

25g/scant 1oz raisins, soaked in water for 2 hours

75g/2½oz roasted almonds and pistachios, finely chopped

1 tbsp caster sugar

Method

- In a bowl, whisk the yoghurt with the saffron.
- Add all the other ingredients. Mix well.
- Serve chilled.

Yam Raita

Serves 4

Ingredients

250g/9oz yams*

Salt to taste

¼ tsp chilli powder

¼ tsp ground black pepper

350g/12oz yoghurt

1 tsp ghee

½ tsp cumin seeds

2 green chillies, slit lengthways

1 tbsp coriander leaves, finely chopped

Method

- Peel and grate the yams. Add some salt and steam the mixture till soft. Set aside.
- In a bowl, mix the salt, chilli powder and ground pepper with the yoghurt.
- Add the yam to the yoghurt mixture. Set aside.
- Heat the ghee in a small saucepan. Add the cumin seeds and green chillies. Let them splutter for 15 seconds.
- Add this to the yoghurt mixture. Mix gently.
- Garnish with the coriander leaves. Serve chilled.

Okra Raita

Serves 4

Ingredients

250g/9oz okra, finely chopped

Salt to taste

½ tsp chilli powder

½ tsp turmeric

Refined vegetable oil for deep frying

350g/12oz yoghurt

1 tsp chaat masala*

Method

- Rub the okra pieces with the salt, chilli powder and turmeric.
- Heat the oil in a saucepan. Deep fry the okra on a medium heat for 3-4 minutes. Drain on absorbent paper. Set aside.
- In a bowl, whisk the yoghurt with the chaat masala and salt.
- Add the fried okra to the yoghurt mixture.
- Serve chilled or at room temperature.

Crunchy Spinach Patty

Makes 12

Ingredients

1 tbsp refined vegetable oil plus extra for deep frying

1 large onion, finely chopped

50g/1¾oz spinach, boiled and finely chopped

1 tsp garlic paste

1 tsp ginger paste

Salt to taste

300g/10oz paneer*, chopped

2 eggs, whisked

2 tbsp plain white flour

Pepper to taste

Salt to taste

50g/1¾oz breadcrumbs

Method

- Heat the oil in a frying pan. Fry the onion on a medium heat till translucent.
- Add the spinach, garlic paste, ginger paste and salt. Cook for 2-3 minutes.

- Remove from the heat and add the paneer. Mix well and divide into square patties. Cover with foil and refrigerate for 30 minutes.
- Mix the eggs, flour, pepper and salt together to form a smooth batter.
- Heat the remaining oil in a frying pan. Dip each paneer patty into the batter, roll in the breadcrumbs and deep fry till golden brown.
- Serve hot with dry garlic chutney

Rava Dosa

(Semolina Crêpe)

Makes 10-12

Ingredients

100g/3½oz semolina

85g/3oz plain white flour

Pinch of bicarbonate of soda

250g/9oz yoghurt

240ml/8fl oz water

Salt to taste

Refined vegetable oil for greasing

Method

- Blend all the ingredients, except the oil, together to form a batter of a pancake-mix consistency. Set aside for 20-30 minutes.
- Grease and heat a flat pan. Pour 2 tbsp of batter in it. Spread by lifting the pan and rotating it gently.
- Pour some oil around the edges.
- Cook for 3 minutes. Flip and cook till crisp.
- Repeat for the remaining batter.
- Serve hot with coconut chutney

Doodhi Cutlet

(Bottle Gourd Cutlet)

Makes 20

Ingredients

1 tbsp refined vegetable oil plus extra for frying

1 large onion, chopped

4 green chillies, finely chopped

2.5cm/1in root ginger, grated

1 large bottle gourd*, peeled and grated

Salt to taste

2 eggs, whisked

100g/3½oz breadcrumbs

For the white sauce:

2 tbsp margarine/butter

4 tbsp flour

Salt to taste

Pepper to taste

1 tbsp cream

Method

- For the white sauce, heat the margarine/butter in a saucepan.
  Add all the remaining white sauce ingredients and stir on a medium heat till thick and creamy. Set aside.
- Heat the oil in a frying pan. Fry the onion, green chillies and ginger on a medium heat for 2-3 minutes.
- Add the bottle gourd and salt. Mix well. Cover with a lid and cook for 15-20 minutes on a medium heat.
- Uncover and mash the bottle gourd well. Add the white sauce and half the whisked eggs. Set aside for 20 minutes to harden and set.
- Chop the mixture into cutlets.
- Heat the oil in a saucepan. Dip each cutlet in the remaining whisked egg, roll in the breadcrumbs and deep fry till golden brown.
- Serve hot with sweet tomato chutney

Patra

(Colocasia Leaf Pinwheel)

Makes 20

Ingredients

10 colocasia leaves*

2 tbsp refined vegetable oil

½ tsp mustard seeds

1 tsp sesame seeds

1 tsp cumin seeds

8 curry leaves

2 tbsp coriander leaves, finely chopped

For the batter:

250g/9oz besan*

4 tbsp jaggery*, grated

1 tsp tamarind paste

½ tsp ginger paste

½ tsp garlic paste

1 tsp chilli powder

½ tsp turmeric

Salt to taste

Method

- Mix all the batter ingredients to form a thick batter.
- Spread a layer of the batter on each colocasia leaf to cover it completely.
- Place 5 coated leaves one above the other.
- Fold the leaves 2.5cm/1in from each corner to form a square. Roll this square into a cylinder.
- Repeat for the other 5 leaves.
- Steam the rolls for about 20-25 minutes. Set aside to cool.
- Slice each roll into pinwheel-like shapes. Set aside.
- Heat the oil in a saucepan. Add the mustard, sesame seeds, cumin seeds and curry leaves. Let them splutter for 15 seconds.
- Pour this over the pinwheels.
- Garnish with the coriander leaves. Serve hot.

Nargisi Chicken Kebab

(Chicken and Cheese Kebab)

Makes 20-25

Ingredients

500g/1lb 2oz chicken, minced

150g/5½oz grated Cheddar cheese

2 large onions, finely chopped

1 tsp ginger paste

1 tsp garlic paste

1 tsp ground cardamom

2 tsp garam masala

1 tsp ground coriander

½ tsp turmeric

½ tsp chilli powder

Salt to taste

15-20 raisins

Refined vegetable oil for deep frying

Method
- Knead all the ingredients, except the raisins and oil, into a dough.
- Make small dumplings. Place a raisin in the centre of each dumpling.
- Heat the oil in a frying pan. Fry the dumplings on a medium heat till golden brown. Serve hot with mint chutney

Sev Puris with Savoury Topping

Serves 4

Ingredients

24 sev puris*

2 potatoes, diced and boiled

1 large onion, finely chopped

¼ small unripe green mango, finely chopped

120ml/4fl oz hot and sour chutney

4 tbsp mint chutney

1 tsp chaat masala*

Juice of 1 lemon

Salt to taste

150g/5½oz sev*

2 tbsp coriander leaves, chopped

Method
- Arrange the puris on a serving plate.
- Place small portions of the potatoes, onion and mango on each puri.
- Sprinkle the hot and sour chutney and mint chutney on top of each puri.
- Sprinkle the chaat masala, lemon juice and salt on top.
- Garnish with the sev and coriander leaves. Serve immediately.

Special Roll

Makes 4

Ingredients

1 tsp yeast

Pinch of sugar

240ml/8fl oz warm water

350g/12oz plain white flour

½ tsp baking powder

2 tbsp butter

1 large onion, finely chopped

2 tomatoes, finely chopped

30g/1oz mint leaves, finely chopped

200g/7oz spinach, boiled

300g/10oz paneer*, diced

Salt to taste

Ground black pepper to taste

125g/4½oz tomato purée

1 egg, whisked

Method

- Dissolve the yeast and sugar in the water.
- Sieve the flour and baking powder together. Mix with the yeast and knead into a dough.
- With a rolling pin, roll out the dough into 2 chapattis. Set aside.
- Heat half the butter in a saucepan. Add the onion, tomatoes, mint leaves, spinach, paneer, salt and black pepper. Sauté on a medium heat for 3 minutes.
- Spread this over 1 chapatti. Pour the tomato purée on top and cover with the other chapatti. Seal the ends.
- Brush the chapattis with the egg and remaining butter.
- Bake in an oven at 150ºC (300ºF, Gas Mark 2) for 10 minutes. Serve hot.

Fried Colocasia

Serves 4

Ingredients

500g/1lb 2 oz colocasia*

2 tbsp ground coriander

1 tbsp ground cumin

1 tbsp amchoor*

2 tsp besan*

Salt to taste

Refined vegetable oil for frying

Chaat masala*, to taste

1 tbsp coriander leaves, chopped

½ tsp lemon juice

Method

- Boil the colocasia in a saucepan for 15 minutes on a low heat. Cool, peel, cut lengthways and flatten. Set aside.
- Mix the ground coriander, ground cumin, amchoor, besan and salt. Roll the colocasia pieces in this mixture. Set aside.
- Heat the oil in a saucepan. Deep fry the colocasia till crisp, then drain.
- Sprinkle with the remaining ingredients. Serve hot.

Mixed Dhal Dosa

(Mixed Lentil Crêpe)

Makes 8-10

Ingredients

250g/9oz rice, soaked for 5-6 hours

100g/3½oz mung dhal*, soaked for 5-6 hours

100g/3½oz chana dhal*, soaked for 5-6 hours

100g/3½oz urad dhal*, soaked for 5-6 hours

2 tbsp yoghurt

½ tsp bicarbonate of soda

2 tbsp refined vegetable oil plus extra for frying

Salt to taste

Method

- Wet grind the rice and the dhals separately. Mix together. Add the yoghurt, bicarbonate of soda, oil and salt. Whisk till fluffy and light. Set aside for 3-4 hours.
- Grease and heat a flat pan. Pour 2 tbsp of batter over it and spread like a crêpe. Pour some oil around the edges. Cook for 2 minutes. Serve hot.

Makkai Cakes

(Corn Cakes)

Makes 12-15

Ingredients

4 fresh corn cobs

2 tbsp butter

750ml/1¼ pints milk

½ tsp chilli powder

Salt to taste

Ground black pepper to taste

25g/scant 1oz coriander leaves, chopped

50g/1¾oz breadcrumbs

Method

- Remove the kernels from the corn cobs and grind them coarsely.
- Heat the butter in a saucepan and fry the ground corn for 2-3 minutes on a medium heat. Add the milk and simmer till dry.
- Add the chilli powder, salt, black pepper and coriander leaves.
- Add the breadcrumbs and mix well. Divide the mixture into small patties.
- Heat the butter in a frying pan. Shallow fry the patties till golden brown. Serve hot with ketchup.

Hara Bhara Kebab

(Green Vegetable Kebab)

Serves 4

Ingredients

300g/10oz chana dhal*, soaked overnight

2 green cardamom pods

2.5cm/1in cinnamon

Salt to taste

60ml/2fl oz water

200g/7oz spinach, steamed and ground

½ tsp garam masala

¼ tsp mace, grated

Refined vegetable oil to shallow fry

Method

- Drain the dhal. Add the cardamom, cloves, cinnamon, salt and water. Cook in a saucepan on a medium heat till soft. Grind to a paste.
- Add all the remaining ingredients, except the oil. Mix well. Divide the mixture into lemon-sized balls and flatten each into small patties.

- Heat the oil in a frying pan. Shallow fry the patties over a medium heat till golden brown. Serve hot with mint chutney

Fish Pakoda

(Battered Fried Fish)

Makes 12

Ingredients

300g/10oz boneless fish, chopped into 2.5cm/1in pieces

Salt to taste

2 tsp lemon juice

3 tbsp water

250g/9oz besan*

1 tsp garlic paste

2 green chillies, finely chopped

1 tsp garam masala

½ tsp turmeric

Refined vegetable oil for deep frying

Method
- Marinate the fish with the salt and lemon juice for 20 minutes.
- Mix the remaining ingredients, except the oil, to make a thick batter.
- Heat the oil in a saucepan. Dip each piece of fish in the batter and fry till golden. Drain on absorbent paper. Serve hot.

Shammi Kebab

(Mince and Bengal Gram Kebab)

Makes 35

Ingredients

750g/1lb 10oz chicken, minced

600g/1lb 5oz chana dhal*

3 large onions, chopped

1 tsp ginger paste

1 tsp garlic paste

2.5cm/1in cinnamon

4 cloves

2 black cardamom pods

7 peppercorns

1 tsp ground cumin

Salt to taste

450ml/15fl oz water

2 eggs, whisked

Refined vegetable oil for frying

Method

- Mix together all the ingredients, except the eggs and oil. Boil in a saucepan till all the water evaporates. Grind to a thick paste.
- Add the eggs to the paste. Mix well. Divide the mixture into 35 patties.
- Heat the oil in a frying pan. Fry the patties on a low heat till golden.
- Serve hot with mint chutney

Basic Dhokla

(Basic Steamed Cake)

Makes 18-20

Ingredients

250g/9oz rice

450g/1lb chana dhal*

60g/2oz yoghurt

¼ tsp bicarbonate of soda

6 green chillies, chopped

1cm/½in root ginger, grated

¼ tsp ground coriander

¼ tsp ground cumin

½ tsp turmeric

Salt to taste

½ coconut, grated

150g/5½oz coriander leaves, finely chopped

1 tbsp refined vegetable oil

½ tsp mustard seeds

Method

- Soak the rice and dhal together for 6 hours. Grind coarsely.
- Add the yoghurt and bicarbonate of soda. Mix well. Let the paste ferment for 6-8 hours.
- Add the green chillies, ginger, ground coriander, ground cumin, turmeric and salt to the batter. Mix thoroughly.
- Pour into a 20cm/8in round cake tin. Steam the batter for 10 minutes.
- Cool and chop into square pieces. Sprinkle the grated coconut and coriander leaves over them. Set aside.
- Heat the oil in a saucepan. Add the mustard seeds. Let them splutter for 15 seconds.
- Pour this over the dhoklas. Serve hot.

Adai

(Rice and Lentil Crêpe)

Makes 12

Ingredients

125g/4½oz rice

75g/2½oz urad dhal*

75g/2½oz chana dhal*

75g/2½oz masoor dhal*

75g/2½oz mung dhal*

6 red chillies

Salt to taste

240ml/8fl oz water

Refined vegetable oil for greasing

Method
- Soak the rice with all the dhals overnight.
- Drain the mixture and add the red chillies, salt and water. Grind until smooth.
- Grease and heat a flat pan. Spread 3 tbsp of the batter on it. Cover and cook on a medium heat for 2-3 minutes. Flip and cook the other side.
- Remove carefully with a spatula. Repeat for the rest of the batter. Serve hot.

Double Decker Dhokla

(Steamed Double Decker Cake)

Makes 20

Ingredients

500g/1lb 2oz rice

300g/10oz urad beans*

75g/2½oz urad dhal*

75g/2½oz chana dhal*

75g/2½oz masoor dhal*

2 green chillies

500g/1lb 2oz yoghurt

1 tsp chilli powder

½ tsp turmeric

Salt to taste

115g/4oz mint chutney

Method

- Mix the rice and urad beans. Soak overnight.
- Mix all the dhals. Soak overnight.
- Drain and grind the rice mixture and the dhal mixture separately. Set aside.
- Mix the green chillies, yoghurt, chilli powder, turmeric and salt together. Add half of this blend to the rice mixture and add the remaining to the dhal mixture. Allow to ferment for 6 hours.
- Grease a 20cm/8in round cake tin. Pour the rice mixture into it. Sprinkle the mint chutney on top of the rice mixture. Pour the dhal mixture on top.
- Steam for 7-8 minutes. Chop and serve hot.

Ulundu Vada

(Fried Doughnut-shaped Snack)

Makes 12

Ingredients

600g/1lb 5oz urad dhal*, soaked overnight and drained

4 green chillies, finely chopped

Salt to taste

3 tbsp water

Refined vegetable oil for deep frying

Method

- Grind the dhal with the green chillies, salt and water.
- Shape the mixture into doughnuts.
- Heat the oil in a saucepan. Add the vadas and deep fry on a medium heat till brown.
- Drain on absorbent paper. Serve hot with coconut chutney

Bhakar Wadi

(Spicy Gram Flour Pinwheel)

Serves 4

Ingredients

500g/1lb 2oz besan*

175g/6oz wholemeal flour

Salt to taste

Pinch of asafoetida

120ml/4fl oz warm refined vegetable oil plus extra for deep frying

100g/3½oz desiccated coconut

1 tsp sesame seeds

1 tsp poppy seeds

Pinch of sugar

1 tsp chilli powder

25g/scant 1oz coriander leaves, finely chopped

1 tbsp tamarind paste

Method

- Knead the besan, flour, salt, asafoetida, warm oil and enough water into a stiff dough. Set aside.

- Dry roast the coconut, sesame seeds and poppy seeds for 3-5 minutes. Grind to a powder.
- Add the sugar, salt, chilli powder, coriander leaves and tamarind paste to the powder and mix thoroughly to prepare the filling. Set aside.
- Divide the dough into lemon-sized balls. Roll each into a thin disc.
- Spread the filling on each disc so that the filling covers the entire disc. Roll each into a tight cylinder. Seal the edges with a little water.
- Slice the cylinders to get pinwheel-like shapes.
- Heat the oil in a saucepan. Add the pinwheel rolls and fry on a medium heat till crisp.
- Drain on absorbent paper. Store in an airtight container once cooled.

NOTE: These can be stored for a fortnight.

Mangalorean Chaat

Serves 4

Ingredients

75g/2½oz chana dhal*

240ml/8fl oz water

Salt to taste

Large pinch of bicarbonate of soda

2 large potatoes, finely chopped and boiled

350g/12oz fresh yoghurt

2 tbsp caster sugar

4 tbsp refined vegetable oil

1 tbsp dried fenugreek leaves

1 tsp ginger paste

1 tsp garlic paste

2 green chillies

1 tsp ground cumin, dry roasted

1 tsp garam masala

1 tbsp amchoor*

1 tsp turmeric

½ tsp chilli powder

150g/5½oz canned chickpeas

1 large onion, finely chopped

2 tbsp coriander leaves, finely chopped

Method

- Cook the dhal with the water, salt and bicarbonate of soda in a saucepan on a medium heat for 30 minutes. Add more water if the dhal feels too dry. Mix the potatoes with the dhal mixture and set aside.
- Whisk the yoghurt with the sugar. Place in the freezer to chill.
- Heat the oil in a saucepan. Add the fenugreek leaves and fry on a medium heat for 3-4 minutes.
- Add the ginger paste, garlic paste, green chillies, ground cumin, garam masala, amchoor, turmeric and chilli powder. Fry for 2-3 minutes, stirring continuously.
- Add the chickpeas. Sauté for 5 minutes, stirring continuously. Add the dhal mixture and mix well.
- Remove from the heat and spread the mixture on a serving platter.
- Pour the sweet yoghurt on top.
- Sprinkle with the onion and coriander leaves. Serve immediately.

Pani Puri

Makes 30

Ingredients
For the puris:

175g/6oz plain white flour

100g/3½oz semolina

Salt to taste

Refined vegetable oil for deep frying

For the stuffing:

50g/1¾oz sprouted mung beans

150g/5½oz sprouted chickpeas

Salt to taste

2 large potatoes, boiled and mashed

For the pani:

2 tbsp tamarind paste

100g/3½oz coriander leaves, finely chopped

1½ tsp ground cumin, dry roasted

2-4 green chillies, finely chopped

2.5cm/1in root ginger

Rock salt to taste

240ml/8fl oz water

Method

- Knead all the puri ingredients, except the oil, with enough water to form a stiff dough.
- Roll out into small puris of 5cm/2in diameter.
- Heat the oil in a frying pan. Deep fry the puris till light brown. Set aside.
- For the stuffing, parboil the sprouted mung beans and chickpeas with the salt. Mix with the potatoes. Set aside.
- For the pani, grind together all the pani ingredients, except the water.
- Add this mixture to the water. Mix well and set aside.
- To serve, make a hole in each puri and fill it with the stuffing. Pour 3 tbsp of the pani into each and serve immediately.

Stuffed Spinach Egg

Serves 4

Ingredients

200g/7oz spinach

Pinch of bicarbonate of soda

1 tbsp refined vegetable oil

1 tsp cumin seeds

6 garlic cloves, crushed

2 green chillies, ground

Salt to taste

8 hard boiled eggs, halved lengthways

1 tbsp ghee

1 onion, finely chopped

2.5cm/1in root ginger, chopped

Method

- Mix the spinach with the bicarbonate of soda. Steam till tender. Grind and set aside.
- Heat the oil in a saucepan. When it begins to smoke, add the cumin seeds, garlic and green chillies. Stir-fry for a few seconds. Add the steamed spinach and salt.
- Cover with a lid and cook till dry. Set aside.
- Scoop the yolks out from the eggs. Add the egg yolks to the spinach mixture. Mix well.
- Place spoonfuls of the spinach-egg mixture in the hollow egg whites. Set aside.
- Heat the ghee in a small frying pan. Fry the onion and ginger till golden brown.
- Sprinkle this on top of the eggs. Serve hot.

Sada Dosa

(Savoury Rice Crêpe)

Makes 15

Ingredients

100g/3½oz parboiled rice

75g/2½oz urad dhal*

½ tsp fenugreek seeds

½ tsp bicarbonate of soda

Salt to taste

125g/4½oz yoghurt, whipped

60ml/2fl oz refined vegetable oil

Method

- Soak the rice and the dhal together with the fenugreek seeds for 7-8 hours.
- Drain and grind the mixture to a grainy paste.
- Add bicarbonate of soda and salt. Mix well.
- Set aside to ferment for 8-10 hours.
- Add the yoghurt to make the batter. This batter should be thick enough to coat a spoon. Add a little water if needed. Set aside.

- Grease and heat a flat pan. Spread a spoonful of the batter over it to make a thin crêpe. Pour 1 tsp oil on top. Cook until crisp. Repeat for the rest of the batter and serve hot.

Potato Samosa

(Potato Savoury)

Makes 20

Ingredients

175g/6oz plain white flour

Pinch of salt

5 tbsp refined vegetable oil plus extra for deep frying

100ml/3½fl oz water

1cm/½in root ginger, grated

2 green chillies, finely chopped

2 garlic cloves, finely chopped

½ tsp ground coriander

1 large onion, finely chopped

2 large potatoes, boiled and mashed

1 tbsp coriander leaves, finely chopped

1 tbsp lemon juice

½ tsp turmeric

1 tsp chilli powder

½ tsp garam masala

Salt to taste

Method

- Mix the flour with the salt, 2 tbsp oil and water. Knead into a pliable dough.
  Cover with a moist cloth and set aside for 15-20 minutes.
- Knead the dough again. Cover with a moist cloth and set aside.
- For the filling, heat 3 tbsp oil in a frying pan. Add the ginger, green chillies, garlic and ground coriander. Fry for a minute on a medium heat, stirring continuously.
- Add the onion and fry till brown.
- Add the potatoes, coriander leaves, lemon juice, turmeric, chilli powder, garam masala and salt. Mix thoroughly.
- Cook on a low heat for 4 minutes, stirring occasionally. Set aside.
- To make the samosas, divide the dough into 10 balls. Roll out into discs of 12cm/5in diameter. Cut each disc into 2 half-moons.
- Run a moist finger along the diameter of a half-moon. Bring the ends together to make a cone.
- Place a tbsp of the filling in the cone and seal by pressing the edges together. Repeat for all the half-moons.
- Heat the oil in a frying pan. Deep fry the samosas, five at a time, over a low heat till light brown. Drain on absorbent paper.
- Serve hot with mint chutney

Hot Kachori

(Fried Dumpling with Lentil Filling)

Makes 15

Ingredients

250g/9oz plain white flour plus 1 tbsp for the patching

5 tbsp refined vegetable oil plus extra for deep frying

Salt to taste

1.4 litres/2½ pints water plus 1 tbsp for patching

300g/10oz mung dhal*, soaked for 30 minutes

½ tsp ground coriander

½ tsp ground fennel

½ tsp cumin seeds

½ tsp mustard seeds

2-3 pinches of asafoetida

1 tsp garam masala

1 tsp chilli powder

Method

- Mix 250g/9oz flour with 3 tbsp oil, salt and 100ml/3½fl oz of the water. Knead into a soft, pliable dough. Set aside for 30 minutes.
- To make the filling, cook the dhal with the remaining water in a saucepan on a medium heat for 45 minutes. Drain and set aside.
- Heat 2 tbsp oil in a saucepan. When it begins to smoke, add the ground coriander, fennel, cumin seeds, mustard seeds, asafoetida, garam masala, chilli powder and salt. Let them splutter for 30 seconds.
- Add the cooked dhal. Mix well and fry for 2-3 minutes, stirring continuously.
- Cool the dhal mixture and divide into 15 lemon-sized balls. Set aside.
- Mix 1 tbsp flour with 1 tbsp water to make a paste for patching. Set aside.
- Divide the dough into 15 balls. Roll out into discs of 12cm/5in diameter.
- Place 1 ball of the filling in the centre of a disc. Seal like a pouch.
- Flatten slightly by pressing it between the palms. Repeat for the remaining discs.
- Heat the oil in a saucepan until it starts smoking. Deep fry the discs till golden brown on the underside. Flip and repeat.
- If a kachori tears while frying, seal it with the patching paste.
- Drain on absorbent paper. Serve hot with mint chutney

Khandvi

(Besan Roll-Ups)

Makes 10-15

Ingredients

60g/2oz besan*

60g/2oz yoghurt

120ml/4fl oz water

1 tsp turmeric

Salt to taste

5 tbsp refined vegetable oil

1 tbsp fresh coconut, grated

1 tbsp coriander leaves, finely chopped

½ tsp mustard seeds

2 pinches of asafoetida

8 curry leaves

2 green chillies, finely chopped

1 tsp sesame seeds

Method

- Mix the besan, yoghurt, water, turmeric and salt together.
- Heat 4 tbsp oil in a frying pan. Add the besan mixture and cook, stirring continuously to make sure no lumps are formed.
- Cook till the mixture leaves the sides of the pan. Set aside.
- Grease two 15 × 35cm/6 × 14in non-stick baking trays. Pour in the besan mixture and smooth flat with a palette knife. Allow to set for 10 minutes.
- Cut the mixture into 5cm/2in wide strips. Carefully roll up each strip.
- Place the rolls in a serving dish. Sprinkle the grated coconut and coriander leaves on top. Set aside.
- Heat 1 tbsp oil in a small saucepan. Add the mustard seeds, asafoetida, curry leaves, green chillies and sesame seeds. Let them splutter for 15 seconds.
- Pour this immediately over the besan rolls. Serve hot or at room temperature.

Makkai Squares

(Corn Squares)

Makes 12

Ingredients

2 tsp ghee

100g/3½oz corn kernels, ground

Salt to taste

125g/4½oz boiled peas

3 tbsp refined vegetable oil

8 green chillies, finely chopped

½ tsp cumin seeds

½ tsp mustard seeds

½ tsp garlic paste

½ tbsp ground coriander

½ tbsp ground cumin

175g/6oz maize flour

175g/6oz wholemeal flour

150ml/5fl oz water

Method

- Heat the ghee in a saucepan. When it begins to smoke, fry the corn for 3 minutes. Set aside.
- Add salt to the boiled peas. Mash the peas well. Set aside.
- Heat 2 tbsp oil in a frying pan. Add the green chillies, cumin and mustard seeds. Let them splutter for 15 seconds.
- Add the fried corn, mashed peas, garlic paste, ground coriander and ground cumin. Mix well. Remove from the heat and set aside.
- Mix both the flours together. Add salt and 1 tbsp oil. Add the water and knead into a soft dough.
- Roll out 24 square shapes, each square 10x10cm/4x4in in size.
- Place the corn and peas mixture in the centre of a square and cover with another square. Gently press the edges of the square to seal.
- Repeat for the rest of the squares.
- Grease and heat a frying pan. Roast the squares on the pan till golden brown.
- Serve hot with ketchup.

Dhal Pakwan

(Crispy Bread with Lentils)

Serves 4

Ingredients

600g/1lb 5oz chana dhal*

3 tbsp refined vegetable oil

1 tsp cumin seeds

750ml/1¼ pints water

Salt to taste

½ tsp turmeric

½ tsp amchoor*

10g/¼oz coriander leaves, finely chopped

For the pakwan:

250g/9oz plain white flour

½ tsp cumin seeds

Salt to taste

Refined vegetable oil for deep frying

Method

- Soak the chana dhal for 4 hours. Drain and set aside.
- Heat the oil in a saucepan. Add the cumin seeds. Let them splutter for 15 seconds.
- Add the soaked dhal, water, salt and turmeric. Simmer for 30 minutes.
- Transfer to a serving dish. Sprinkle with the amchoor and coriander leaves. Set aside.
- Knead all the pakwan ingredients, except the oil, with enough water to make a stiff dough.
- Divide into walnut-sized balls. Roll out into thick discs, 10cm/4in in diameter. Pierce all over with a fork.
- Heat the oil in a frying pan. Deep fry the discs till golden. Drain on absorbent paper.
- Serve the pakwans with the hot dhal.

Spicy Sev

(Spicy Gram Flour Flakes)

Serves 4

Ingredients

500g/1lb 2oz besan*

1 tsp ajowan seeds

1 tbsp refined vegetable oil plus extra for deep frying

¼ tsp asafoetida

Salt to taste

200ml/7fl oz water

Method

- Knead the besan with the ajowan seeds, oil, asafoetida, salt and water into a sticky dough.
- Put the dough in a piping bag.
- Heat the oil in a saucepan. Press the dough through the nozzle in the form of noodles into the pan and fry lightly on both sides.
- Drain well and cool before storing.

NOTE: *This can be stored for a fortnight.*

Stuffed Veggie Crescents

Makes 6

Ingredients

350g/12oz plain white flour

6 tbsp warm refined vegetable oil plus extra for deep frying

Salt to taste

1 tomato, sliced

For the filling:

3 tbsp refined vegetable oil

200g/7oz peas

1 carrot, julienned

100g/3½oz French beans, chopped into thin strips

4 tbsp fresh coconut, grated

3 green chillies

2.5cm/1in root ginger, crushed

4 tsp coriander leaves, finely chopped

2 tsp sugar

2 tsp lemon juice

Salt to taste

Method

- First make the filling. Heat the oil in a saucepan. Add the peas, carrot and French beans and fry, stirring continuously, till soft.
- Add all the remaining filling ingredients and mix well. Set aside.
- Mix the flour with the oil and the salt. Knead into a stiff dough.
- Divide the dough into 6 lemon-sized balls.
- Roll each ball into a disc of 10cm/4in diameter.
- Place the vegetable filling on one half of a disc. Fold the other half over to cover the filling and press the edges together to seal.
- Repeat for all the discs.
- Heat the oil in a saucepan. Add the crescents and fry till they are golden brown.
- Arrange them in a round serving dish and garnish with the tomato slices. Serve immediately.

Kachori Usal

(Fried Bread with Chickpeas)

Serves 4

Ingredients
For the pastry:

50g/1¾oz fenugreek leaves finely chopped

175g/6oz wholemeal flour

2 green chillies, finely chopped

1 tsp ginger paste

¼ tsp turmeric

100ml/3½fl oz water

Salt to taste

For the filling:

1 tsp refined vegetable oil

250g/9oz mung beans, boiled

250g/9oz green chickpeas, boiled

¼ tsp turmeric

½ tsp chilli powder

1 tsp ground coriander

1 tsp ground cumin

Salt to taste

For the sauce:

2 tsp refined vegetable oil

2 large onions, finely chopped

2 tomatoes, chopped

1 tsp garlic paste

½ tsp garam masala

¼ tsp chilli powder

Salt to taste

Method

- Mix all the pastry ingredients together. Knead into a firm dough. Set aside.
- For the filling, heat the oil in a frying pan and sauté all the filling ingredients on a medium heat for 5 minutes. Set aside.
- For the sauce, heat the oil in a frying pan. Add all the sauce ingredients. Fry for 5 minutes, stirring occasionally. Set aside.
- Divide the dough into 8 portions. Roll out each portion into a disc of 10cm/4in diameter.
- Place some filling in the centre of a disc. Seal like a pouch and smooth to form a stuffed ball. Repeat for all the discs.

- Steam the balls for 15 minutes.
- Add the balls to the sauce and toss to coat. Cook on a low heat for 5 minutes.
- Serve hot.

Dhal Dhokli

(Gujarati Savoury Snack)

Serves 4

Ingredients
For the dhokli:

175g/6oz wholemeal flour

Pinch of turmeric

¼ tsp chilli powder

½ tsp ajowan seeds

1 tsp refined vegetable oil

100ml/3½fl oz water

For the dhal:

2 tbsp refined vegetable oil

3-4 cloves

5cm/2in cinnamon

1 tsp mustard seeds

300g/10oz masoor dhal*, cooked and mashed

½ tsp turmeric

Pinch of asafoetida

1 tbsp tamarind paste

2 tbsp grated jaggery*

60g/2oz peanuts

1 tsp ground coriander

1 tsp ground cumin

½ tsp chilli powder

Salt to taste

25g/scant 1oz coriander leaves, finely chopped

Method

- Mix all the dhokli ingredients together. Knead to form a firm dough.
- Divide the dough into 5-6 balls. Roll out into thick discs, 6cm/2.4in in diameter. Set aside for 10 minutes to harden.
- Cut out the dhokli discs into diamond-shaped pieces. Set aside.
- For the dhal, heat the oil in a saucepan. Add the cloves, cinnamon and mustard seeds. Let them splutter for 15 seconds.
- Add all the remaining dhal ingredients, except the coriander leaves. Mix well. Cook on a high heat till the dhal starts boiling.
- Add the dhokli pieces to the boiling dhal. Continue to cook over a low heat for 10 minutes.
- Garnish with the coriander leaves. Serve hot.

Misal

(Healthy Sprouted Beans Snack)

Serves 4

Ingredients

3-4 tbsp refined vegetable oil

½ tsp mustard seeds

¼ tsp asafoetida

6 curry leaves

1 tsp ginger paste

1 tsp garlic paste

25g/scant 1oz coriander leaves, ground in a blender

1 tsp chilli powder

1 tsp tamarind paste

2 tsp grated jaggery*

Salt to taste

300g/10oz sprouted mung beans, boiled

2 large potatoes, diced and boiled

500ml/16fl oz water

300g/10oz Bombay Mix*

1 large tomato, finely chopped

1 large onion, finely chopped

25g/scant 1oz coriander leaves, finely chopped

4 slices of bread

For the spice mixture:

1 tsp cumin seeds

2 tsp coriander seeds

2 cloves

3 peppercorns

¼ tsp ground cinnamon

Method

- Grind together all the ingredients of the spice mixture. Set aside.
- Heat the oil in a saucepan. Add the mustard seeds, asafoetida and curry leaves. Let them splutter for 2-3 minutes.
- Add the ginger paste, garlic paste, ground coriander leaves, chilli powder, tamarind paste, jaggery and salt. Mix well and cook for 3-4 minutes.
- Add the ground spice mixture. Sauté for 2-3 minutes.
- Add the sprouted beans, potatoes and water. Mix well and simmer for 15 minutes.
- Transfer to a serving bowl and sprinkle with the Bombay Mix, chopped tomato, chopped onion and coriander leaves on top.
- Serve hot with a slice of bread on the side.

Pandori

(Mung Dhal Snack)

Makes 12

Ingredients

1 green chilli, halved lengthways

Salt to taste

1 tsp bicarbonate of soda

¼ tsp asafoetida

250g/9oz whole mung dhal*, soaked for 4 hours

2 tsp refined vegetable oil

2 tsp coriander leaves, finely chopped

Method

- Add the green chilli, salt, bicarbonate of soda and asafoetida to the dhal. Grind to a paste.
- Grease a 20cm/8in round cake tin with the oil and pour the dhal paste in it. Steam for 10 minutes.
- Set the steamed dhal mixture aside for 10 minutes. Once cool, cut into 2.5cm/1in pieces.
- Garnish with the coriander leaves. Serve hot with green coconut chutney

Vegetable Adai

(Vegetable, Rice and Lentil Crêpe)

Makes 8

Ingredients

100g/3½oz parboiled rice

150g/5½oz masoor dhal*

75g/2½oz urad dhal*

3-4 red chillies

¼ tsp asafoetida

Salt to taste

4 tbsp water

1 onion, finely chopped

½ carrot, finely chopped

50g/1¾oz cabbage,

finely chopped 4-5 curry leaves

10g/¼oz coriander leaves, finely chopped

4 tsp refined vegetable oil

Method

- Soak the rice and the dhals together for about 20 minutes.
- Drain and add the red chillies, asafoetida, salt and water. Grind to a coarse paste.
- Add the onion, carrot, cabbage, curry leaves and coriander leaves. Mix well to make a batter with a consistency similar to sponge cake batter. Add more water if the consistency is not right.
- Grease a flat pan. Pour a spoonful of the batter. Spread with the back of a spoon to make a thin crêpe.
- Pour half a tsp oil around the crêpe. Flip to cook both sides.
- Repeat for the rest of the batter. Serve hot with coconut chutney

Spicy Corn on the Cob

Serves 4

Ingredients

8 corn cobs

Salted butter to taste

Salt to taste

2 tsp chaat masala*

2 lemons, halved

Method

- Roast the corns cobs on a charcoal grill or open flame till golden brown all over.
- Rub the butter, salt, chaat masala and the lemons on each cob.
- Serve immediately.

Mixed Vegetable Chop

Makes 12

Ingredients

Salt to taste

¼ tsp ground black pepper

4-5 large potatoes, boiled and mashed

2 tbsp refined vegetable oil plus extra for deep frying

1 small onion, finely chopped

½ tsp garam masala

1 tsp lemon juice

100g/3½oz frozen mixed vegetables

2-3 green chillies, finely chopped

50g/1¾oz coriander leaves, finely chopped

250g/9oz arrowroot powder

150ml/5fl oz water

100g/3½oz breadcrumbs

Method

- Add the salt and black pepper to the potatoes. Mix well and divide into 12 balls. Set aside.
- For the filling, heat 2 tbsp oil in a frying pan. Fry the onion on a medium heat till translucent.
- Add the garam masala, lemon juice, mixed vegetables, green chillies and coriander leaves. Mix well and cook on a medium heat for 2-3 minutes. Mash well and set aside.
- Flatten the potato balls with greased palms.
- Place some filling mixture on eacn potato patty. Seal to make oblong-shaped chops. Set aside.
- Mix the arrowroot powder with enough water to form a thin batter.
- Heat the oil in a frying pan. Dip the chops in the batter, roll in the breadcrumbs and deep fry on a medium heat till golden brown.
- Drain and serve hot.

Idli Upma

(Steamed Rice Cake Snack)

Serves 4

Ingredients

5 tbsp refined vegetable oil

½ tsp mustard seeds

½ tsp cumin seeds

1 tsp urad dhal*

2 green chillies, slit lengthways

8 curry leaves

Pinch of asafoetida

¼ tsp turmeric

8 idlis crushed

2 tsp caster sugar

1 tbsp coriander leaves, finely chopped

Salt to taste

Method

- Heat the oil in a saucepan. Add the mustard seeds, cumin seeds, urad dhal, green chillies, curry leaves, asafoetida and turmeric. Let them splutter for 30 seconds.
- Add the crushed idlis, caster sugar, coriander and salt. Mix gently.
- Serve immediately.

Dhal Bhajiya

(Batter Fried Lentil Balls)

Makes 15

Ingredients

250/9oz mung dhal*, soaked for 2-3 hours

2 green chillies, finely chopped

2 tbsp coriander leaves, finely chopped

1 tsp cumin seeds

Salt to taste

Refined vegetable oil for deep frying

Method

- Drain the dhal and grind coarsely.
- Add the chillies, coriander leaves, cumin seeds and salt. Mix well.
- Heat the oil in a frying pan. Add small portions of the dhal mixture and fry over a medium heat till golden brown.
- Serve hot with mint chutney

Masala Papad

(Poppadoms Topped with Spices)

Makes 8

Ingredients

2 tomatoes, finely chopped

2 large onions, finely chopped

3 green chillies, finely chopped

10g/¼oz coriander leaves, chopped

2 tsp lemon juice

1 tsp chaat masala*

Salt to taste

8 poppadoms

Method

- Mix all the ingredients, except the poppadoms, in a bowl.
- Roast the poppadoms on a high heat, turning each side. Make sure you don't burn them.
- Spread the vegetable mixture over each poppadom. Serve immediately.

Vegetable Sandwich

Makes 6

Ingredients

12 bread slices

50g/1¾oz butter

100g/3½oz mint chutney

1 large potato, boiled and thinly sliced

1 tomato, thinly sliced

1 large onion, thinly sliced

1 cucumber, thinly sliced

Chaat masala* to taste

Salt to taste

Method

- Butter the bread slices and apply a thin coat of mint chutney on each.
- Place a layer of potato, tomato, onion and cucumber slices on 6 bread slices.
- Sprinkle with some chaat masala and salt.
- Cover with the remaining bread slices and cut as desired. Serve immediately.

Sprouted Mung Bean Rolls

Makes 8

Ingredients

175g/6oz wholemeal flour

2 tbsp plain white flour

½ tsp caster sugar

75ml/ 2½fl oz water

50g/1¾oz frozen peas

25g/scant 1oz sprouted mung beans

2 tbsp refined vegetable oil

50g/1¾oz spinach, finely chopped

1 small tomato, finely chopped

1 small onion, finely chopped

30g/1oz cabbage leaves, finely chopped

1 tsp ground cumin

1 tsp ground coriander

¼ tsp ginger paste

¼ tsp garlic paste

60ml/2fl oz cream

Salt to taste

750g/1lb 10oz yoghurt

Method

- Mix the wholemeal flour, plain white flour, sugar and water. Knead into a stiff dough. Set aside.
- Boil the peas and mung beans in minimum water. Drain and set aside.
- Heat the oil in a saucepan. Add the spinach, tomato, onion and cabbage. Fry, stirring occasionally, till the tomato turns pulpy.
- Add the peas and mung beans mixture along with all remaining ingredients, except the dough. Cook on a medium heat till dry. Set aside.
- Make thin chapattis with the dough.
- On one side of each chapatti, place the cooked mixture lengthways in the centre, and roll up. Serve with mint chutney and yoghurt.

Chutney Sandwich

Makes 6

Ingredients

12 bread slices

½ tsp butter

6 tbsp mint chutney

4 tomatoes, sliced

Method

- Butter all the bread slices. Spread the mint chutney on 6 slices.
- Place the tomatoes over the mint chutney and cover with another buttered slice. Serve immediately.

Chatpata Gobhi

(Tangy Cauliflower Snack)

Serves 4

Ingredients

500g/1lb 2oz cauliflower florets

Salt to taste

1 tsp ground black pepper

1 tbsp refined vegetable oil

1 tbsp lemon juice

Method

- Steam the cauliflower florets for 10 minutes. Set aside to cool.
- Mix the steamed florets thoroughly with the remaining ingredients. Spread the cauliflower on a flameproof dish and grill for 5-7 minutes, or till it turns brown. Serve hot.

Sabudana Vada

(Sago Cutlet)

Makes 12

Ingredients

300g/10oz sago

125g/4½oz peanuts, roasted and crushed coarsely

2 large potatoes, boiled and mashed

5 green chillies, crushed

Salt to taste

Refined vegetable oil for deep frying

Method

- Soak the sago for 5 hours. Drain thoroughly and set aside for 3-4 hours.
- Mix the sago with all the ingredients, except the oil. Knead well.
- Grease your palms and make twelve patties with the mixture.
- Heat the oil in a frying pan. Deep fry 3-4 patties at a time on a medium heat till golden brown.
- Drain on absorbent paper. Serve hot with mint chutney.

Bread Upma

(Bread Snack)

Serves 4

Ingredients

2 tbsp refined vegetable oil

½ tsp mustard seeds

½ tsp cumin seeds

3 green chillies, slit lengthways

½ tsp turmeric

¼ tsp asafoetida

2 onions, finely chopped

2 tomatoes, finely chopped

Salt to taste

2 tsp sugar

3-4 tbsp water

15 bread slices, broken into bits

1 tbsp coriander leaves, chopped

Method

- Heat the oil in a frying pan. Add the mustard seeds, cumin seeds, green chillies, turmeric and asafoetida. Let them splutter for 15 seconds.
- Add the onions and sauté till translucent. Add the tomatoes, salt, sugar and water. Bring to boil on a medium heat.
- Add the bread and mix well. Simmer for 2-3 minutes, stirring occasionally.
- Garnish with the coriander leaves. Serve hot.

Spicy Khaja

(Spicy Flour Dumplings with Ginger)

Makes 25-30

Ingredients

500g/1lb 2oz besan*

85g/3oz plain white flour

2 tsp chilli powder

½ tsp ajowan seeds

½ tsp cumin seeds

1 tbsp coriander leaves, chopped

Salt to taste

200ml/7fl oz water

1 tbsp refined vegetable oil plus extra for deep frying

Method

- Knead all the ingredients, except the oil for frying, into a soft dough.

- Make 25-30 balls of 10cm/4in diameter. Prick all over with a fork.

- Allow to dry on a clean cloth for 25-30 minutes.

- Deep fry till golden brown. Drain, cool and store for up to 15 days.

Crispy Potato

Serves 4

Ingredients

500g/1lb 2oz Greek yoghurt

1 tsp ginger paste

1 tsp garlic paste

1 tsp garam masala

1 tsp ground cumin, dry roasted

1 tbsp mint leaves, chopped

½ tbsp coriander leaves, chopped

Salt to taste

2 tbsp refined vegetable oil

4-5 potatoes, peeled and julienned

Method

- Whisk the yoghurt in a bowl. Add all the ingredients, except the oil and the potatoes. Mix well.

- Marinate the potatoes with the yoghurt for 3-4 hours in the refrigerator.

- Pour the oil in a grilling pan and arrange the marinated potatoes on it.

- Grill for 10 minutes. Turn the potatoes and grill for another 8-10 minutes till crispy. Serve hot.

Dhal Vada

(Fried Mixed Lentil Patties)

Makes 15

Ingredients

300g/10oz whole masoor dhal*

150g/5½oz masoor dhal*

1 large onion, finely chopped

2.5cm/1in root ginger, finely chopped

3 green chillies, finely chopped

¼ tbsp asafoetida

Salt to taste

Refined vegetable oil for frying

Method

- Mix the dhals together. Place in a colander and pour water in them. Set aside for an hour. Pat dry with a towel.

- Grind the dhals into a paste. Add all the remaining ingredients, except the oil. Mix well and shape the mixture into patties.

- Heat the oil in a frying pan. Deep fry the patties on a medium heat till golden brown. Serve hot with mint chutney

Batter Fried Shrimp

Serves 4

Ingredients

250g/9oz shrimps, peeled

250g/9oz besan*

2 green chillies, finely chopped

1 tsp chilli powder

1 tsp turmeric

1 tsp ground coriander

1 tsp ground cumin

½ tsp amchoor*

1 small onion, grated

¼ tsp bicarbonate of soda

Salt to taste

Refined vegetable oil for deep frying

Method
- Mix together all the ingredients, except the oil, with enough water to form a thick batter.
- Heat the oil in a pan. Drop a few spoonfuls of the batter in it and fry on a medium heat till golden on all sides.
- Repeat for the remaining batter. Serve hot.

Mackerel in Tomato Gravy

Serves 4

Ingredients

1 tbsp refined vegetable oil

2 large onions, finely chopped

2 tomatoes, finely chopped

1 tbsp ginger paste

1 tbsp garlic paste

1 tsp chilli powder

½ tsp turmeric

8 dry kokum*

2 green chillies, sliced

Salt to taste

4 large mackerel, skinned and filleted

120ml/4fl oz water

Method
- Heat the oil in a saucepan. Fry the onions on a medium heat till brown. Add all the remaining ingredients, except the fish and water. Mix well and sauté for 5-6 minutes.
- Add the fish and water. Mix well. Simmer for 15 minutes and serve hot.

Konju Ullaruathu

(Scampi in Red Masala)

Serves 4

Ingredients

120ml/4fl oz refined vegetable oil

1 large onion, finely chopped

5cm/2in root ginger, finely sliced

12 garlic cloves, finely sliced

2 tbsp green chillies, finely chopped

8 curry leaves

2 tomatoes, finely chopped

1 tsp turmeric

2 tsp ground coriander

1 tsp ground fennel

600g/1lb 5oz scampi, shelled and de-veined

3 tsp chilli powder

Salt to taste

1 tsp garam masala

Method

- Heat the oil in a saucepan. Add the onion, ginger, garlic, green chillies and curry leaves and fry on a medium heat for 1-2 minutes.
- Add all the remaining ingredients, except the garam masala. Mix well and cook on a low heat for 15-20 minutes.
- Sprinkle with the garam masala and serve hot.

Chemeen Manga Curry

(Curried Prawns with Unripe Mango)

Serves 4

Ingredients

200g/7oz fresh coconut, grated

1 tbsp chilli powder

2 large onions, finely sliced

3 tbsp refined vegetable oil

2 green chillies, chopped

2.5cm/1in root ginger, thinly sliced

Salt to taste

1 tsp turmeric

1 small unripe mango, diced

120ml/4fl oz water

750g/1lb 10oz tiger prawns, shelled and de-veined

1 tsp mustard seeds

10 curry leaves

2 whole red chillies

4-5 shallots, sliced

Method

- Grind together the coconut, chilli powder and half the onions. Set aside.
- Heat half the oil in a saucepan. Sauté the remaining onions with the green chillies, ginger, salt and turmeric on a low heat for 3-4 minutes.
- Add the coconut paste, unripe mango and water. Simmer for 8 minutes.
- Add the prawns. Simmer for 10-12 minutes and set aside.
- Heat the remaining oil. Add the mustard seeds, curry leaves, chillies and shallots. Fry for a minute. Add this mixture to the prawns and serve hot.

Simple Machchi Fry

(Fish fried with Spices)

Serves 4

Ingredients

8 fillets of firm white fish such as cod

¾ tsp turmeric

½ tsp chilli powder

1 tsp lemon juice

250ml/8fl oz refined vegetable oil

2 tbsp plain white flour

Method

- Marinate the fish with the turmeric, chilli powder and lemon juice for 1 hour.
- Heat the oil in a frying pan. Coat the fish with the flour and shallow fry on a medium heat for 3-4 minutes. Flip and fry for 2-3 minutes. Serve hot.

Machher Kalia

(Fish in Rich Gravy)

Serves 4

Ingredients

1 tsp coriander seeds

2 tsp cumin seeds

1 tsp chilli powder

2.5cm/1in root ginger, peeled

250ml/8fl oz water

120ml/4fl oz refined vegetable oil

500g/1lb 2oz trout fillets, skinned

3 bay leaves

1 large onion, finely chopped

4 garlic cloves, finely chopped

4 green chillies, sliced

Salt to taste

1 tsp turmeric

2 tbsp yoghurt

Method

- Grind the coriander seeds, cumin seeds, chilli powder and ginger with enough water to form a thick paste. Set aside.
- Heat the oil in a saucepan. Add the fish and fry on a medium heat for 3-4 minutes. Flip and repeat. Drain and set aside.
- To the same oil, add the bay leaves, onion, garlic and green chillies. Fry for 2 minutes. Add the remaining ingredients, the fried fish and the paste. Mix well and simmer for 15 minutes. Serve hot.

Fish Fried in Egg

Serves 4

Ingredients

500g/1lb 2oz John Dory, skinned and filleted

Juice of 1 lemon

Salt to taste

2 eggs

1 tbsp plain white flour

½ tsp ground black pepper

1 tsp chilli powder

250ml/8fl oz refined vegetable oil

100g/3½oz breadcrumbs

Method

- Marinate the fish with the lemon juice and salt for 4 hours.
- Whisk the eggs with the flour, pepper and chilli powder.
- Heat the oil in a frying pan. Dip the marinated fish in the egg mixture, roll in the breadcrumbs and fry on a low heat till golden brown. Serve hot.

Lau Chingri

(Shrimps with Pumpkin)

Serves 4

Ingredients

250g/9oz shrimps, peeled

500g/1lb 2oz pumpkin, diced

2 tbsp mustard oil

¼ tsp cumin seeds

1 bay leaf

½ tsp turmeric

1 tbsp ground coriander

¼ tsp sugar

1 tbsp milk

Salt to taste

Method

- Steam the shrimps and pumpkin together for 15-20 minutes. Set aside.
- Heat the oil in a saucepan. Add the cumin seeds and bay leaf. Fry for 15 seconds. Add the turmeric and ground coriander. Fry on a medium heat for 2-3 minutes. Add the sugar, milk, salt and the steamed shrimps and pumpkin. Simmer for 10 minutes. Serve hot.

Tomato Fish

Serves 4

Ingredients

2 tbsp plain white flour

1 tsp ground black pepper

500g/1lb 2oz lemon sole, skinned and filleted

3 tbsp butter

2 bay leaves

1 small onion, grated

6 garlic cloves, finely chopped

2 tsp lemon juice

6 tbsp fish stock

150g/5½oz tomato purée

Salt to taste

Method

- Mix the flour and pepper together. Toss the fish in the mixture.
- Heat the butter in a frying pan. Fry the fish on a medium heat till golden. Drain and set aside.
- In the same butter, fry the bay leaves, onion and garlic on a medium heat for 2-3 minutes. Add the fried fish and all the remaining ingredients. Mix well and simmer for 20 minutes. Serve hot.

Chingri Machher Kalia

(Rich Prawn Curry)

Serves 4

Ingredients

24 large prawns, shelled and de-veined

½ tsp turmeric

Salt to taste

250ml/8fl oz water

3 tbsp mustard oil

2 large onions, finely grated

6 dry red chillies, ground

2 tbsp coriander leaves, finely chopped

Method

- Cook the prawns with the turmeric, salt and water in a saucepan on a medium heat for 20-25 minutes. Set aside. Do not discard the water.
- Heat the oil in a saucepan. Add the onions and red chillies and fry on a medium heat for 2-3 minutes.
- Add the cooked prawns and the reserved water. Mix well and simmer for 20-25 minutes. Garnish with the coriander leaves. Serve hot.

Fish Tikka Kebab

Serves 4

Ingredients

1 tbsp malt vinegar

1 tbsp yoghurt

1 tsp ginger paste

1 tsp garlic paste

2 green chillies, finely chopped

1 tsp garam masala

1 tsp ground cumin

1 tsp chilli powder

Dash of orange food colouring

Salt to taste

675g/1½lb monkfish, skinned and filleted

Method

- Mix together all the ingredients, except the fish. Marinate the fish with this mixture for 3 hours.
- Arrange the marinated fish on skewers and grill for 20 minutes. Serve hot.

Vegetable Patties

Makes 12

Ingredients

2 tbsp arrowroot powder

4-5 large potatoes, boiled and grated

1 tbsp refined vegetable oil plus extra for frying

125g/4½oz besan*

25g/scant 1oz fresh coconut, grated

4-5 cashew nuts

3-4 raisins

125g/4½oz frozen peas, boiled

2 tsp dried pomegranate seeds

2 tsp coarsely ground coriander

1 tsp fennel seeds

½ tsp ground black pepper

½ tsp chilli powder

1 tsp amchoor*

½ tsp rock salt

Salt to taste

Method

- Knead together the arrowroot, potatoes and 1 tbsp of oil. Set aside.

- To make the filling, mix the remaining ingredients, except the oil.

- Divide the potato dough into round patties. Place a spoonful of the filling in the centre of each patty. Seal them like a pouch and flatten.

- Heat the remaining oil in a saucepan. Shallow fry the patties over a low heat till golden brown. Serve hot.

Sprouted Beans Bhel

(Savoury Snack with Sprouted Beans)

Serves 4

Ingredients

100g/3½oz sprouted mung beans, boiled

250g/9oz kaala chana*, boiled

3 large potatoes, boiled and chopped

2 large tomatoes, finely chopped

1 medium-sized onion, chopped

Salt to taste

For the garnish:

2 tbsp mint chutney

2 tbsp hot and sweet mango chutney

4-5 tbsp yoghurt

100g/3½ oz potato crisps, crushed

10g/¼oz coriander leaves, chopped

Method
- Mix all the ingredients together, except the garnish ingredients.
- Garnish in the order that the ingredients are listed. Serve immediately.

Aloo Kachori

(Fried Potato Dumpling)

Makes 15

Ingredients

350g/12oz wholemeal flour

1 tbsp refined vegetable oil plus extra for deep frying

1 tsp ajowan seeds

Salt to taste

5 potatoes, boiled and mashed

2 tsp chilli powder

1 tbsp coriander leaves, chopped

Method

- Knead the flour, 1 tbsp oil, ajowan seeds and salt together. Divide into lime-sized balls. Flatten each between your palms and set aside.
- Mix together the potatoes, chilli powder, coriander leaves and some salt.
- Place a portion of this mixture in the centre of each patty. Seal by pinching the edges together.
- Heat the oil in a frying pan. Deep fry the kachoris on a medium heat till golden brown. Drain and serve hot.

Diet Dosa

(Diet Crêpe)

Makes 12

Ingredients

300g/10oz mung dhal*, soaked in 250ml/8fl oz water for 3-4 hours

3-4 green chillies

2.5cm/1in root ginger

100g/3½oz semolina

1 tbsp sour cream

50g/1¾oz coriander leaves, chopped

6 curry leaves

Refined vegetable oil for greasing

Salt to taste

Method

- Mix the dhal with the green chillies and ginger. Grind together.
- Add the semolina and sour cream. Mix well. Add the coriander leaves, curry leaves and enough water to make a thick batter.

- Grease a flat pan and heat it. Pour 2 tbsp batter on it and spread with the back of a spoon. Cook for 3 minutes on a low heat. Flip and repeat.
- Repeat for the remaining batter. Serve hot.

Nutri Roll

Makes 8-10

Ingredients

200g/7oz spinach, finely chopped

1 carrot, finely chopped

125g/4½oz frozen peas

50g/1¾oz sprouted mung beans

3-4 large potatoes, boiled and mashed

2 large onions, finely chopped

½ tsp ginger paste

½ tsp garlic paste

1 green chilli, finely chopped

½ tsp amchoor*

Salt to taste

½ tsp chilli powder

3 tbsp coriander leaves, finely chopped

Refined vegetable oil for shallow frying

8-10 chapattis

2 tbsp hot and sweet mango chutney

Method

- Steam the spinach, carrots, peas and mung beans together.
- Mix the steamed vegetables with the potatoes, onions, ginger paste, garlic paste, green chilli, amchoor, salt, chilli powder and coriander leaves. Knead well to make a smooth mixture.
- Shape the mixture into small cutlets.
- Heat the oil in a saucepan. Shallow fry the cutlets on a medium heat till golden brown. Drain and set aside.
- Spread some hot and sweet mango chutney over a chapatti. Place a cutlet in the centre and roll the chapatti up.
- Repeat for all the chapattis. Serve hot.

Sabudana Palak Doodhi Uttapam

(Sago, Spinach and Bottle Gourd Pancake)

Makes 20

Ingredients

1 tsp toor dhal*

1 tsp mung dhal*

1 tsp urad beans*

1 tsp masoor dhal*

3 tsp rice

100g/3½ oz sago, coarsely ground

50g/1¾oz spinach, steamed and ground

¼ bottle gourd*, grated

125g/4½oz besan*

½ tsp ground cumin

1 tsp mint leaves, finely chopped

1 green chilli, finely chopped

½ tsp ginger paste

Salt to taste

100ml/3½fl oz water

Refined vegetable oil for frying

Method
- Grind together the toor dhal, mung dhal, urad beans, masoor dhal and rice. Set aside.
- Soak the sago for 3-5 minutes. Drain completely.
- Mix with the ground dhal-and-rice mixture.
- Add the spinach, bottle gourd, besan, ground cumin, mint leaves, green chilli, ginger paste, salt and enough water to make a thick batter. Set aside for 30 minutes.
- Grease a frying pan and heat it. Pour 1 tbsp batter in the pan and spread it with the back of a spoon.
- Cover and cook on a medium heat till the underside is light brown. Flip and repeat.
- Repeat for the remaining batter. Serve hot with tomato ketchup or green coconut chutney

Poha

Serves 4

Ingredients

150g/5½oz poha*

1½ tbsp refined vegetable oil

½ tsp cumin seeds

½ tsp mustard seeds

1 large potato, finely chopped

2 large onions, finely sliced

5-6 green chillies, finely chopped

8 curry leaves, roughly chopped

¼ tsp turmeric

45g/1½oz roasted peanuts (optional)

25g/scant 1oz fresh coconut, grated or scraped

10g/¼oz coriander leaves, finely chopped

1 tsp lemon juice

Salt to taste

Method

- Wash the poha well. Drain the water completely and set the poha aside in a colander for 15 minutes.
- Gently loosen the poha lumps with your fingers. Set aside.
- Heat the oil in a saucepan. Add the cumin and mustard seeds. Let them splutter for 15 seconds.
- Add the chopped potatoes. Stir-fry on a medium heat for 2-3 minutes. Add the onions, green chillies, curry leaves and turmeric. Cook till the onions are translucent. Remove from the heat.
- Add the poha, roasted peanuts and half of the grated coconut and coriander leaves. Toss to mix thoroughly.
- Sprinkle the lemon juice and salt. Cook on a low heat for 4-5 minutes.
- Garnish with the remaining coconut and coriander leaves. Serve hot.

Vegetable Cutlet

Makes 10-12

Ingredients

2 onions, finely chopped

5 garlic cloves

¼ tsp fennel seeds

2-3 green chillies

10g/¼oz coriander leaves, finely chopped

2 large carrots, finely chopped

1 large potato, finely chopped

1 small beetroot, finely chopped

50g/1¾oz French beans, finely chopped

50g/1¾oz green peas

900ml/1½ pints water

Salt to taste

¼ tsp turmeric

2-3 tbsp besan*

1 tbsp refined vegetable oil plus extra for deep frying

50g/1¾oz breadcrumbs

Method

- Grind 1 onion, the garlic, fennel seeds, green chillies and coriander leaves together into a smooth paste. Set aside.
- Mix the carrots, potato, beetroot, French beans and peas together in a saucepan. Add 500ml/16fl oz water, salt and turmeric and cook on a medium heat till the vegetables are soft.
- Mash the vegetables thoroughly and set aside.
- Mix the besan and the remaining water together to form a smooth batter. Set aside.
- Heat 1 tbsp oil in a saucepan. Add the remaining onion and fry till translucent.
- Add the onion-garlic paste and fry for a minute on a medium heat, stirring continuously.
- Add the mashed vegetables and mix thoroughly.
- Remove from the heat and set aside to cool.
- Divide this mixture into 10-12 balls. Flatten between your palms to make patties.
- Dip the patties in the batter and roll in the breadcrumbs.
- Heat the oil in a frying pan. Shallow fry the patties till golden brown on both sides.
- Serve hot with ketchup.

Soy Bean Uppit

(Soy Bean Snack)

Serves 4

Ingredients

1½ tbsp refined vegetable oil

½ tsp mustard seeds

2 green chillies, finely chopped

2 red chillies, finely chopped

Pinch of asafoetida

1 large onion, finely chopped

2.5cm/1in root ginger, julienned

10 garlic cloves, finely chopped

6 curry leaves

100g/3½oz soy bean semolina*, dry roasted

100g/3½oz semolina, dry roasted

200g/7oz peas

500ml/16fl oz hot water

¼ tsp turmeric

1 tsp sugar

1 tsp salt

1 large tomato, finely chopped

2 tbsp coriander leaves, finely chopped

15 raisins

10 cashew nuts

Method

- Heat the oil in a saucepan. Add the mustard seeds. Let them splutter for 15 seconds.
- Add the green chillies, red chillies, asafoetida, onion, ginger, garlic and curry leaves. Fry on a medium heat for 3-4 minutes, stirring frequently.
- Add the soy bean semolina, semolina and the peas. Cook till both the kinds of the semolina turn golden brown.
- Add the hot water, turmeric, sugar and salt. Cook over a medium heat till the water dries up.
- Garnish with the tomato, coriander leaves, raisins and cashew nuts.
- Serve hot.

Upma

(Semolina Breakfast Dish)

Serves 4

Ingredients

1 tbsp ghee

150g/5½oz semolina

1 tbsp refined vegetable oil

¼ tsp mustard seeds

1 tsp urad dhal*

3 green chillies, slit lengthways

8-10 curry leaves

1 medium-sized onion, finely chopped

1 medium-sized tomato, finely chopped

750ml/1¼ pints water

1 heaped tsp sugar

Salt to taste

50g/1¾oz canned peas (optional)

25g/scant 1oz coriander leaves, finely chopped

Method

- Heat the ghee in a frying pan. Add the semolina and fry, stirring frequently, till the semolina turns golden brown. Set aside.
- Heat the oil in a saucepan. Add the mustard seeds, urad dhal, green chillies and curry leaves. Fry till the urad dhal turns brown.
- Add the onion and fry on a low heat till translucent. Add the tomato and fry for another 3-4 minutes.
- Add the water and mix well. Cook on a medium heat till the mixture starts boiling. Stir well.
- Add the sugar, salt, semolina and peas. Mix well.
- Cook on a low heat, stirring continuously for 2-3 minutes.
- Garnish with the coriander leaves. Serve hot.

Vermicelli Upma

(Vermicelli with Onion)

Serves 4

Ingredients

3 tbsp refined vegetable oil

1 tsp mung dhal*

1 tsp urad dhal*

¼ tsp mustard seeds

8 curry leaves

10 peanuts

10 cashew nuts

1 medium potato, finely chopped

1 large carrot, finely chopped

2 green chillies, finely chopped

1cm/½ in root ginger, finely chopped

1 large onion, finely chopped

1 tomato, finely chopped

50g/1¾oz frozen peas

Salt to taste

1 litre/1¾ pints water

200g/7oz vermicelli

2 tbsp ghee

Method

- Heat the oil in a saucepan. Add the mung dhal, urad dhal, mustard seeds and curry leaves. Let them splutter for 30 seconds.
- Add the peanuts and cashew nuts. Fry on a medium heat till golden brown.
- Add the potato and carrot. Fry for 4-5 minutes.
- Add the chillies, ginger, onion, tomato, peas and salt. Cook on a medium heat, stirring frequently, till the vegetables are tender.
- Add the water and bring to a boil. Stir well.
- Add the vermicelli while stirring continuously to make sure no lumps are formed.
- Cover with a lid and cook on a low heat for 5-6 minutes.
- Add the ghee and mix well. Serve hot.

Bonda

(Potato Chop)

Makes 10

Ingredients

5 tbsp refined vegetable oil plus extra for deep frying

½ tsp mustard seeds

2.5mm/1in root ginger, finely chopped

2 green chillies, finely chopped

50g/1¾oz coriander leaves, finely chopped

1 large onion, finely chopped

4 medium-sized potatoes, boiled and mashed

1 large carrot, finely chopped and boiled

125g/4½oz canned peas

Pinch of turmeric

Salt to taste

1 tsp lemon juice

250g/9oz besan*

200ml/7fl oz water

½ tsp baking powder

Method

- Heat 4 tbsp oil in a saucepan. Add the mustard seeds, ginger, green chillies, coriander leaves and onion. Fry on a medium heat, stirring occasionally, till the onion turns brown.
- Add the potatoes, carrot, peas, turmeric and salt. Cook on a low heat for 5-6 minutes, stirring occasionally.
- Sprinkle lemon juice and divide the mixture into 10 balls. Set aside.
- Mix the the besan, water and baking powder with 1 tbsp oil to make the batter.
- Heat the oil in a saucepan. Dip each potato ball in the batter and deep fry on a medium heat till golden brown.
- Serve hot.

Instant Dhokla

(Instant Steamed Savoury Cake)

Makes 15-20

Ingredients

250g/9oz besan*

1 tsp salt

2 tbsp sugar

2 tbsp refined vegetable oil

½ tbsp lemon juice

240ml/8fl oz water

1 tbsp baking powder

1 tsp mustard seeds

2 green chillies, slit lengthways

A few curry leaves

1 tbsp water

2 tbsp coriander leaves, finely chopped

1 tbsp fresh coconut, grated

Method

- Mix together the besan, salt, sugar, 1 tbsp oil, lemon juice and water to make a smooth batter.
- Grease a 20cm/8in round cake tin.
- Add the baking powder to the batter. Mix well and pour immediately in the greased tin. Steam for 20 minutes.
- Pierce with a fork to check if done. If the fork does not come out clean, steam again for 5-10 minutes. Set aside.
- Heat the remaining oil in a saucepan. Add the mustard seeds. Let them splutter for 15 seconds.
- Add the green chillies, curry leaves and water. Cook on a low heat for 2 minutes.
- Pour this mixture over the dhokla and allow it to soak up the liquid.
- Garnish with the coriander leaves and grated coconut.
- Cut into squares and serve with mint chutney

Dhal Maharani

(Black Lentils and Kidney Beans)

Serves 4

Ingredients

150g/5½oz urad dhal*

2 tbsp kidney beans

1.4 litres/2½ pints water

Salt to taste

1 tbsp refined vegetable oil

½ tsp cumin seeds

1 large onion, finely chopped

3 medium-sized tomatoes, chopped

1 tsp ginger paste

½ tsp garlic paste

½ tsp chilli powder

½ tsp garam masala

120ml/4fl oz fresh single cream

Method

- Soak the urad dhal and kidney beans together overnight. Drain and cook together in a saucepan with the water and salt for 1 hour on a medium heat. Set aside.
- Heat the oil in a saucepan. Add the cumin seeds. Let them splutter for 15 seconds.
- Add the onion and fry on a medium heat till golden brown.
- Add the tomatoes. Mix well. Add the ginger paste and garlic paste. Fry for 5 minutes.
- Add the cooked dhal and beans mixture, chilli powder and garam masala. Mix well.
- Add the cream. Simmer for 5 minutes, stirring frequently.
- Serve hot with naan or steamed rice

Milagu Kuzhambu

(Split Red Gram in a Pepper Sauce)

Serves 4

Ingredients

2 tsp ghee

2 tsp coriander seeds

1 tbsp tamarind paste

1 tsp ground black pepper

¼ tsp asafoetida

Salt to taste

1 tbsp toor dhal*, cooked

1 litre/1¾ pints water

¼ tsp mustard seeds

1 green chilli, chopped

¼ tsp turmeric

10 curry leaves

Method

- Heat a few drops of ghee in a saucepan. Add the coriander seeds and fry on a medium heat for 2 minutes. Cool and grind.
- Mix with the tamarind paste, pepper, asafoetida, salt and dhal in a large saucepan.
- Add the water. Mix well and bring to a boil on a medium heat. Set aside.
- Heat the remaining ghee in a saucepan. Add the mustard seeds, green chilli, turmeric and curry leaves. Let them splutter for 15 seconds.
- Add this to the dhal. Serve hot.

Dhal Hariyali

(Leafy Vegetables with Split Bengal Gram)

Serves 4

Ingredients

300g/10oz toor dhal*

1.4 litres/2½ pints water

Salt to taste

2 tbsp ghee

1 tsp cumin seeds

1 onion, finely chopped

½ tsp ginger paste

½ tsp garlic paste

½ tsp turmeric

50g/1¾oz spinach, chopped

10g/¼oz fenugreek leaves, finely chopped

25g/scant 1oz coriander leaves

Method

- Cook the dhal with the water and salt in a saucepan for 45 minutes, stirring frequently. Set aside.
- Heat the ghee in a saucepan. Add the cumin seeds, onion, ginger paste, garlic paste and turmeric. Fry for 2 minutes on a low heat, stirring continuously.
- Add the spinach, fenugreek leaves and the coriander leaves. Mix well and simmer for 5-7 minutes.
- Serve hot with steamed rice

Dhalcha

(Split Bengal Gram with Lamb)

Serves 4

Ingredients

150g/5½oz chana dhal*

150g/5½oz toor dhal*

2.8 litres/5 pints water

Salt to taste

2 tbsp tamarind paste

2 tbsp refined vegetable oil

4 large onions, chopped

5cm/2in root ginger, grated

10 garlic cloves, pounded

750g/1lb 10oz lamb, chopped

1.4 litres/2½ pints water

3-4 tomatoes, chopped

1 tsp chilli powder

1 tsp turmeric

1 tsp garam masala

20 curry leaves

25g/scant 1oz coriander leaves, finely chopped

Method

- Cook the dhals with the water and salt for 1 hour on a medium heat. Add the tamarind paste and mash well. Set aside.
- Heat the oil in a saucepan. Add the onions, ginger and garlic. Fry on a medium heat till brown. Add the lamb and stir constantly till brown.
- Add water and simmer till the lamb is tender.
- Add the tomatoes, chilli powder, turmeric and salt. Mix well. Cook for another 7 minutes.
- Add the dhal, garam masala and curry leaves. Mix well. Simmer for 4-5 minutes.
- Garnish with the coriander leaves. Serve hot.

Tarkari Dhalcha

(Split Bengal Gram with Vegetables)

Serves 4

Ingredients

150g/5½oz chana dhal*

150g/5½oz toor dhal*

Salt to taste

3 litres/5¼ pints water

10g/¼oz mint leaves

10g/¼oz coriander leaves

2 tbsp refined vegetable oil

½ tsp mustard seeds

½ tsp cumin seeds

Pinch of fenugreek seeds

Pinch of kalonji seeds*

2 dry red chillies

10 curry leaves

½ tsp ginger paste

½ tsp garlic paste

½ tsp turmeric

1 tsp chilli powder

1 tsp tamarind paste

500g/1lb 2oz pumpkin, finely diced

Method

- Cook both the dhals with the salt, 2.5 litres/4 pints of water and half the mint and coriander in a saucepan on a medium heat for 1 hour. Grind into a thick paste. Set aside.
- Heat the oil in a saucepan. Add the mustard, cumin, fenugreek and kalonji seeds. Let them splutter for 15 seconds.
- Add the red chillies and curry leaves. Fry on a medium heat for 15 seconds.
- Add the dhal paste, ginger paste, garlic paste, turmeric, chilli powder and tamarind paste. Mix well. Cook on a medium heat, stirring frequently, for 10 minutes.
- Add the remaining water and the pumpkin. Simmer till the pumpkin is cooked.
- Add the remaining mint and coriander leaves. Cook for 3-4 minutes.
- Serve hot.

Dhokar Dhalna

(Fried Dhal Cubes in Curry)

Serves 4

Ingredients

600g/1lb 5oz chana dhal*, soaked overnight

120ml/4fl oz water

Salt to taste

4 tbsp refined vegetable oil plus extra for deep frying

3 green chillies, chopped

½ tsp asafoetida

2 large onions, finely chopped

1 bay leaf

1 tsp ginger paste

1 tsp garlic paste

1 tsp chilli powder

¾ tsp turmeric

1 tsp garam masala

1 tbsp coriander leaves, finely chopped

Method

- Grind the dhal with the water and some salt to a thick paste. Set aside.
- Heat 1 tbsp oil in a saucepan. Add the green chillies and asafoetida. Let them splutter for 15 seconds. Stir in the dhal paste and some more salt. Mix well.
- Spread this mixture on a tray to cool. Cut into 2.5cm/1in pieces.
- Heat the oil for deep frying in a saucepan. Fry the pieces till golden brown. Set aside.
- Heat 2 tbsp oil in a saucepan. Fry the onions till brown. Grind them to a paste and set aside.
- Heat the remaining 1 tbsp oil in a saucepan. Add the bay leaf, fried dhal pieces, the fried onion paste, ginger paste, garlic paste, chilli powder, turmeric and garam masala. Add enough water to cover the dhal pieces. Mix well and simmer for 7-8 minutes.
- Garnish with the coriander leaves. Serve hot.

Varan

(Simple Split Red Gram Dhal)

Serves 4

Ingredients

300g/10oz toor dhal*

2.4 litres/4 pints water

¼ tsp asafoetida

½ tsp turmeric

Salt to taste

Method

- Cook all the ingredients in a saucepan for about 1 hour on a medium heat.
- Serve hot with steamed rice

Sweet Dhal

(Sweet Split Red Gram)

Serves 4-6

Ingredients

300g/10oz toor dhal*

2.5 litres/4 pints water

Salt to taste

¼ tsp turmeric

A large pinch of asafoetida

½ tsp chilli powder

5cm/2in piece of jaggery*

2 tsp refined vegetable oil

¼ tsp cumin seeds

¼ tsp mustard seeds

2 dry red chillies

1 tbsp coriander leaves, finely chopped

Method

- Wash and cook the toor dhal with the water and salt in a saucepan on a low heat for 1 hour.
- Add the turmeric, asafoetida, chilli powder, and jaggery. Cook for 5 minutes. Mix thoroughly. Set aside.
- In a small saucepan, heat the oil. Add the cumin seeds, mustard seeds and the dry red chillies. Let them splutter for 15 seconds.
- Pour this in the dhal and mix well.
- Garnish with the coriander leaves. Serve hot.

Sweet & Sour Dhal

(Sweet and Sour Split Red Gram)

Serves 4-6

Ingredients

300g/10oz toor dhal*

2.4 litres/4 pints water

Salt to taste

¼ tsp turmeric

¼ tsp asafoetida

1 tsp tamarind paste

1 tsp sugar

2 tsp refined vegetable oil

½ tsp mustard seeds

2 green chillies

8 curry leaves

1 tbsp coriander leaves, finely chopped

Method

- Cook the toor dhal in a saucepan with the water and salt on a medium heat for 1 hour.
- Add the turmeric, asafoetida, tamarind paste and sugar. Cook for 5 minutes. Set aside.
- In a small saucepan, heat the oil. Add the mustard seeds, green chillies and curry leaves. Let them splutter for 15 seconds.
- Pour this seasoning in the dhal.
- Garnish with the coriander leaves.
- Serve hot with steamed rice or chapattis

Mung-ni-Dhal

(Split Green Gram)

Serves 4

Ingredients

300g/10oz mung dhal*

1.9 litres/3½ pints water

Salt to taste

¼ tsp turmeric

½ tsp ginger paste

1 green chilli, finely chopped

¼ tsp sugar

1 tbsp ghee

½ tsp sesame seeds

1 small onion, chopped

1 garlic clove, chopped

Method

- Boil the mung dhal with the water and salt in a saucepan on a medium heat for 30 minutes.
- Add the turmeric, ginger paste, green chilli and sugar. Stir well.
- Add 120ml/4fl oz water if the dhal is dry. Simmer for 2-3 minutes and set aside.
- Heat the ghee in a small saucepan. Add the sesame seeds, onion and garlic. Fry them for 1 minute, stirring continuously.
- Add this to the dhal. Serve hot.

Dhal with Onion & Coconut

(Split Red Gram with Onion and Coconut)

Serves 4-6

Ingredients

300g/10oz toor dhal*

2.8 litres/5 pints water

2 green chillies, chopped

1 small onion, chopped

Salt to taste

¼ tsp turmeric

1½ tsp vegetable oil

½ tsp mustard seeds

1 tbsp coriander leaves, finely chopped

50g/1¾oz fresh coconut, grated

Method

- Boil the toor dhal with water, green chillies, onion, salt and turmeric in a saucepan on a medium heat for 1 hour. Set aside.
- Heat the oil in a saucepan. Add the mustard seeds. Let them splutter for 15 seconds.
- Pour this in the dhal and mix well.
- Garnish with the coriander leaves and coconut. Serve hot.

Dahi Kadhi

(Yoghurt-based Curry)

Serves 4

Ingredients

1 tbsp besan*

250g/9oz yoghurt

750ml/1¼ pints water

2 tsp sugar

Salt to taste

½ tsp ginger paste

1 tbsp refined vegetable oil

¼ tsp mustard seeds

¼ tsp cumin seeds

¼ tsp fenugreek seeds

8 curry leaves

10g/¼oz coriander leaves, finely chopped

Method

- Mix the besan with the yoghurt, water, sugar, salt and ginger paste in a large saucepan. Stir well to make sure no lumps form.
- Cook the mixture on a medium heat till it starts to thicken, stirring frequently. Bring to the boil. Set aside.
- Heat the oil in a saucepan. Add the mustard seeds, cumin seeds, fenugreek seeds and curry leaves. Let them splutter for 15 seconds.
- Pour this oil on top of the besan mixture.
- Garnish with the coriander leaves. Serve hot.

Spinach Dhal

(Spinach with Split Green Gram)

Serves 4

Ingredients

300g/10oz mung dhal*

1.9 litres/3½ pints water

Salt to taste

1 large onion, chopped

6 garlic cloves, chopped

¼ tsp turmeric

100g/3½oz spinach, chopped

½ tsp amchoor*

Pinch of garam masala

½ tsp ginger paste

1 tbsp refined vegetable oil

1 tsp cumin seeds

2 tbsp coriander leaves, finely chopped

Method

- Cook the dhal with the water and salt in a saucepan on a medium heat for 30-40 minutes.
- Add the onion and garlic. Cook for 7 minutes.
- Add the turmeric, spinach, amchoor, garam masala and ginger paste. Mix thoroughly.
- Simmer till the dhal is soft and all the spices have been absorbed. Set aside.
- Heat the oil in a saucepan. Add the cumin seeds. Let them splutter for 15 seconds.
- Pour this on top of the dhal.
- Garnish with the coriander leaves. Serve hot

Tawker Dhal

(Sour Split Red Lentil with Unripe Mango)

Serves 4

Ingredients

300g/10oz toor dhal*

2.4 litres/4 pints water

1 unripe mango, stoned and quartered

½ tsp turmeric

4 green chillies

Salt to taste

2 tsp mustard oil

½ tsp mustard seeds

1 tbsp coriander leaves, finely chopped

Method

- Boil the dhal with the water, mango pieces, turmeric, green chillies and salt for an hour. Set aside.
- Heat the oil in a saucepan and add the mustard seeds. Let them splutter for 15 seconds.
- Add this to the dhal. Simmer till thick.
- Garnish with the coriander leaves.
  Serve hot with steamed rice

Basic Dhal

(Split Red Gram with Tomato)

Serves 4

Ingredients

300g/10oz toor dhal*

1.2 litres/2 pints water

Salt to taste

¼ tsp turmeric

½ tbsp refined vegetable oil

¼ tsp cumin seeds

2 green chillies, slit lengthways

1 medium-sized tomato, finely chopped

1 tbsp coriander leaves, finely chopped

Method

- Cook the toor dhal with the water and salt in a saucepan for 1 hour on a medium heat.
- Add the turmeric and mix well.
- If the dhal is too thick, add 120ml/4fl oz water to it. Mix well and set aside.
- Heat the oil in a saucepan. Add the cumin seeds and let them splutter for 15 seconds. Add the green chillies and tomato. Fry for 2 minutes.
- Add this to the dhal. Mix and simmer for 3 minutes.
- Garnish with the coriander leaves. Serve hot with steamed rice

Maa-ki-Dhal

(Rich Black Gram)

Serves 4

Ingredients

240g kaali dhal*

125g/4½oz kidney beans

2.8 litres/5 pints water

Salt to taste

3.5cm/1½in root ginger, julienned

1 tsp chilli powder

3 tomatoes, puréed

1 tbsp butter

2 tsp refined vegetable oil

1 tsp cumin seeds

2 tbsp single cream

Method

- Soak the dhal and the kidney beans together overnight.
- Cook with the water, salt and ginger in a saucepan for 40 minutes on a medium heat.
- Add the chilli powder, tomato purée and butter. Simmer for 8-10 minutes. Set aside.
- Heat the oil in a saucepan. Add the cumin seeds. Let them splutter for 15 seconds.
- Add this to the dhal. Mix well.
- Add the cream. Serve hot with steamed rice

Dhansak

(Spicy Parsi Split Red Gram)

Serves 4

Ingredients

3 tbsp refined vegetable oil

1 large onion, finely chopped

2 large tomatoes, chopped

½ tsp turmeric

½ tsp chilli powder

1 tbsp dhansak masala*

1 tbsp malt vinegar

Salt to taste

For the dhal mixture:

150g/5½oz toor dhal*

75g/2½oz mung dhal*

75g/2½oz masoor dhal*

1 small aubergine, quartered

7.5cm/3in piece of pumpkin, quartered

1 tbsp fresh fenugreek leaves

1.4 litres/2½ pints water

Salt to taste

Method

- Cook the ingredients for the dhal mixture together in a saucepan on a medium heat for 45 minutes. Set aside.
- Heat the oil in a saucepan. Fry the onions and tomatoes on a medium heat for 2-3 minutes.
- Add the dhal mixture and all the remaining ingredients. Mix well and cook on a medium heat for 5-7 minutes. Serve hot.

Masoor Dhal

Serves 4

Ingredients

300g/10oz masoor dhal*

Salt to taste

Pinch of turmeric

1.2 litres/2 pints water

2 tbsp refined vegetable oil

6 garlic cloves, crushed

1 tsp lemon juice

Method

- Cook the dhal, salt, turmeric and water in a saucepan on a medium heat for 45 minutes. Set aside.
- Heat the oil in a frying pan and fry the garlic till brown. Add to the dhal and sprinkle with the lemon juice. Mix well. Serve hot.

Panchemel Dhal

(Five Lentil Mix)

Serves 4

Ingredients

75g/2½oz mung dhal*

1 tbsp chana dhal*

1 tbsp masoor dhal*

1 tbsp toor dhal*

1 tbsp urad dhal*

750ml/1¼ pints water

½ tsp turmeric

Salt to taste

1 tbsp ghee

1 tsp cumin seeds

Pinch of asafoetida

½ tsp garam masala

1 tsp ginger paste

Method

- Cook the dhals with the water, turmeric and salt in a saucepan for 1 hour on a medium heat. Stir well. Set aside.
- Heat the ghee in a saucepan. Fry the remaining ingredients for 1 minute.
- Add this to the dhal, mix well and simmer for 3-4 minutes. Serve hot.

Cholar Dhal

(Split Bengal Gram)

Serves 4

Ingredients

600g/1lb 5oz chana dhal*

2.4 litres/5 pints water

Salt to taste

3 tbsp ghee

½ tsp cumin seeds

½ tsp turmeric

2 tsp sugar

3 cloves

2 bay leaves

2.5cm/1in cinnamon

2 green cardamom pods

15g/½oz coconut, chopped and fried

Method

- Cook the dhal with the water and salt in a saucepan on a medium heat for 1 hour. Set aside.
- Heat 2 tbsp ghee in a saucepan. Add all the ingredients, except the coconut. Let them splutter for 20 seconds. Add the cooked dhal and cook, stirring well for 5 minutes. Add the coconut and 1 tbsp ghee. Serve hot.

Dilpasand Dhal

(Special Lentils)

Serves 4

Ingredients

60g/2oz urad beans*

2 tbsp kidney beans

2 tbsp chickpeas

2 litres/3½ pints water

¼ tsp turmeric

2 tbsp ghee

2 tomatoes, blanched and puréed

2 tsp ground cumin, dry roasted

125g/4½oz yoghurt, whisked

120ml/4fl oz single cream

Salt to taste

Method

- Mix both the beans, chickpeas and water. Soak in a saucepan for 4 hours. Add the turmeric and cook for 45 minutes on a medium heat. Set aside.
- Heat the ghee in a saucepan. Add all the remaining ingredients and cook on a medium heat till the ghee separates.
- Add the beans and chickpeas mixture. Simmer till dry. Serve hot.

Dhal Masoor

(Split Red Lentils)

Serves 4

Ingredients

1 tbsp ghee

1 tsp cumin seeds

1 small onion, finely chopped

2.5cm/1in root ginger, finely chopped

6 garlic cloves, finely chopped

4 green chillies, slit lengthways

1 tomato, peeled and puréed

½ tsp turmeric

300g/10oz masoor dhal*

1.5 litres/2¾ pints water

Salt to taste

2 tbsp coriander leaves

Method

- Heat the ghee in a saucepan. Add the cumin seeds, onion, ginger, garlic, chillies, tomato and turmeric. Fry for 5 minutes, stirring frequently.
- Add the dhal, water and salt. Simmer for 45 minutes. Garnish with the coriander leaves. Serve hot with steamed rice

Dhal with Aubergine

(Lentils with Aubergine)

Serves 4

Ingredients

300g/10oz toor dhal*

1.5 litre/2¾ pints water

Salt to taste

1 tbsp refined vegetable oil

50g/1¾oz aubergines, diced

2.5cm/1in cinnamon

2 green cardamom pods

2 cloves

1 large onion, finely chopped

2 large tomatoes, finely chopped

½ tsp ginger paste

½ tsp garlic paste

1 tsp ground coriander

½ tsp turmeric

10g/¼oz coriander leaves, to garnish

Method

- Boil the dhal with the water and salt in a saucepan for 45 minutes on a medium heat. Set aside.
- Heat the oil in a saucepan. Add all the remaining ingredients, except the coriander leaves. Fry for 2-3 minutes, stirring constantly.
- Add the mixture to the dhal. Simmer for 5 minutes. Garnish and serve.

Yellow Dhal Tadka

Serves 4

Ingredients

300g/10oz mung dhal*

1 litre/1¾ pints water

¼ tsp turmeric

Salt to taste

3 tsp ghee

½ tsp mustard seeds

½ tsp cumin seeds

½ tsp fenugreek seeds

2.5cm/1in root ginger, finely chopped

4 garlic cloves, finely chopped

3 green chillies, slit lengthways

8 curry leaves

Method

- Cook the dhal with the water, turmeric and salt in a saucepan for 45 minutes on a medium heat. Set aside.
- Heat the ghee in a saucepan. Add all the remaining ingredients. Fry them for 1 minute and pour on top of the dhal. Mix well and serve hot.

Rasam

(Spicy Tamarind-based Soup)

Serves 4

Ingredients

2 tbsp tamarind paste

750ml/1¼ pints water

8-10 curry leaves

2 tbsp chopped coriander leaves

Pinch of asafoetida

Salt to taste

2 tsp ghee

½ tsp mustard seeds

For the spice mixture:

2 tsp coriander seeds

2 tbsp toor dhal*

1 tsp cumin seeds

4-5 peppercorns

1 dried red chilli

Method

- Dry roast and grind the spice mixture ingredients together.
- Mix the spice mixture with all the ingredients, except the ghee and the mustard seeds. Cook for 7 minutes on a medium heat in a saucepan.
- Heat the ghee in another saucepan. Add the mustard seeds and let them splutter for 15 seconds. Pour this directly in the rasam. Serve hot.

Simple Mung Dhal

Serves 4

Ingredients

300g/10oz mung dhal*

1 litre/1¾ pints water

Pinch of turmeric

Salt to taste

2 tbsp refined vegetable oil

1 large onion, finely chopped

3 green chillies, finely chopped

2.5cm/1in root ginger, finely chopped

5 curry leaves

2 tomatoes, finely chopped

Method

- Cook the dhal with the water, turmeric and salt in a saucepan for 30 minutes on a medium heat. Set aside.
- Heat the oil in a saucepan. Add all the remaining ingredients. Fry for 3-4 minutes. Add this to the dhal. Simmer till thick. Serve hot.

Whole Green Mung

Serves 4

Ingredients

250g/9oz mung beans, soaked overnight

1 litre/1¾ pints water

½ tbsp refined vegetable oil

½ tsp cumin seeds

6 curry leaves

1 large onion, finely chopped

½ tsp garlic paste

½ tsp ginger paste

3 green chillies, finely chopped

1 tomato, finely chopped

¼ tsp turmeric

Salt to taste

120ml/4fl oz milk

Method

- Cook the beans with the water in a saucepan for 45 minutes on a medium heat. Set aside.
- Heat the oil in a saucepan. Add the cumin seeds and curry leaves.
- After 15 seconds, add the cooked beans and all the remaining ingredients. Mix well and simmer for 7-8 minutes. Serve hot.

Dahi Kadhi with Pakoras

(Yoghurt-based Curry with Fried Dumplings)

Serves 4

Ingredients
For the pakora:

125g/4½oz besan*

¼ tsp cumin seeds

2 tsp chopped onions

1 chopped green chilli

½ tsp grated ginger

Pinch of turmeric

2 green chillies, finely chopped

½ tsp ajowan seeds

Salt to taste

Oil for deep frying

For the kadhi:

Dahi Kadhi

Method

- In a bowl, mix all the pakora ingredients, except the oil, with enough water to form a thick batter. Fry spoonfuls in hot oil till golden brown.
- Cook the kadhi and add the pakoras to it. Simmer for 3-4 minutes.
- Serve hot with steamed rice

Sweet Unripe Mango Dhal

(Split Red Gram with Unripe Mango)

Serves 4

Ingredients

300g/10oz toor dhal*

2 green chillies, slit lengthways

2 tsp jaggery*, grated

1 small onion, sliced

Salt to taste

¼ tsp turmeric

1.5 litres/2¾ pints water

1 unripe mango, peeled and chopped

1½ tsp refined vegetable oil

½ tsp mustard seeds

1 tbsp coriander leaves, for garnish

Method

- Mix all the ingredients, except the oil, mustard seeds and coriander leaves, in a saucepan. Cook for 30 minutes on a medium heat. Set aside.
- Heat the oil in a saucepan. Add the mustard seeds. Let them splutter for 15 seconds. Pour this on top of the dhal. Garnish and serve hot.

Malai Dhal

(Split Black Gram with Cream)

Serves 4

Ingredients

300g/10oz urad dhal*, soaked for 4 hours

1 litre/1¾ pints water

500ml/16fl oz milk, boiled

1 tsp turmeric

Salt to taste

½ tsp amchoor*

2 tbsp single cream

1 tbsp ghee

1 tsp cumin seeds

2.5cm/1in root ginger, finely chopped

1 small tomato, finely chopped

1 small onion, finely chopped

Method

- Cook the dhal with the water on a medium heat for 45 minutes.
- Add the milk, turmeric, salt, amchoor and cream. Mix well and cook for 3-4 minutes. Set aside.
- Heat the ghee in a saucepan. Add the cumin seeds, ginger, tomato and onion. Fry for 3 minutes. Add this to the dhal. Mix well and serve hot.

www.ingramcontent.com/pod-product-compliance
Lightning Source LLC
Chambersburg PA
CBHW071820080526
44589CB00012B/862